FINGERTIP FACTS for the 1956 CHEVROLET

Motorbooks International
Publishers & Wholesalers ®

First published in 1994 by Motorbooks International Publishers & Wholesalers, PO Box 2, 729 Prospect Avenue, Osceola, WI 54020 USA

Motorbooks International books are also available at discounts in bulk quantity for industrial or sales-promotional use. For details write to Special Sales Manager at the Publisher's address

Library of Congress Cataloging-in-Publication Data
Fingertip facts for the 1956 Chevrolet / Damon Enterprises.
      p.   cm.
   ISBN 0-87938-851-X
   1. Chevrolet automobile—Specifications.   2. Chevrolet automobile—History.   I. Damon Enterprises.   II. Title. 1956 Chevrolet.
      TL215.C48F562 1994
      629.222′2—dc20   93-33476

Printed and bound in the United States of America

A WHOLE KIT OF SELLING TOOLS... AND HOW TO USE IT!

This is *your* book. Everything about it was planned to help *you* close deals. If you examine it closely, you will find that it is a whole kit of selling tools that can be used in many ways to point out Chevrolet's superiorities. To make it easy for you to use, it was made small enough to fit your brief case, your coat pocket, and the glove compartment of your demonstrator, yet large enough to give you full product information.

All the information your prospects will want to know about the 1956 Chevrolet is included. Every statement or figure is a fact that has been fully verified by Chevrolet engineers. Each fact is expressed in simple language. All facts on any item are in one place, under one heading, with adjacent marginal notes to direct your eyes swiftly to the one you want. The items are grouped in fourteen sections (see *Table of Contents*). The first two and the last two are *special sections:* the intermediate ten are *feature sections.* The illustrated text of the sections is intended to add to your selling conversation and to give you a refresher course on hard-to-remember points. It also can be shown to prospects who like to see printed facts. Tabs on the first pages of all sections give you fingertip access to any section. In addition, the tabbed page of a *feature section,* and its opposite page, list all the important features in the section. Together, these pages comprise *a complete list of Chevrolet features,* which you can use, without need to refer to the text, to tell your prospect a complete product story.

Associated features of the car are grouped in the *feature sections;* and each section is complete in that it covers accessory and

Sections

Text

Tabs

Feature
Pages

Feature
Sections

optional as well as standard equipment. The individual interests of your prospects will determine which you should use.

Color Chips

Color chips and charts are shown in a four-page insert in the *Exteriors* section. Its pages are not numbered so you may place it where you wish. The *Engines* section is divided into two parts, one for the V8's; one for the Six.

Engines

Special Sections

The car as a whole is considered in each of the four *special sections*. The one entitled *1956 Chevrolet* gives a quick overall impression of the line of cars. It includes a chart that lists the principal specifications of all postwar Chevrolets so you can tell a prospect who owns an older model Chevrolet about the size and power advantages newer Chevrolets (1956 or used) have that his car lacks.

1956 Chevrolet

Models

Individual two-page spreads in the *Models* section enable you to concentrate on selling the main features and specifications of any particular model in which your prospect is interested. If he is undecided about which model he wants, a chart (in *Interiors*) enables you to point out the differences in standard equipment between models. Another chart lists all extra-cost equipment.

All the facts you need to know in a hurry are repeated in *Fast Facts*, in condensed form and in *alphabetical* sequence. In addition, the index for all Chevrolet information is combined with this factual data to give you a quick reference to the text for detailed information. Definitions also are included. To answer the prospect who may also be interested in competitive cars, the *Competition* section (complete with its own index) gives information that may convince him the Chevrolet is the "better buy."

Fast Facts

Competition

In this book, we have tried to give you the finest kit of selling tools in the industry. If, however, you can tell us how to make next year's book even better, we will be glad to consider your suggestions and comments carefully. Please send them to Facts Editor, Chevrolet Sales Promotion Department, General Motors Bldg., Detroit 2, Michigan.

Your Ideas Will Help

New Hardtops and Station Wagons

- ADDED Bel Air Sport Sedan
  —4-door hardtop
- ADDED "Two-Ten" Sport Sedan
  —4-door hardtop
- ADDED "Two-Ten" Sport Coupe*
  —2-door hardtop
- ADDED Bel Air Nomad*
  —Special 2-door station wagon
- ADDED Bel Air Beauville
  —9-passenger station wagon
- ADDED "Two-Ten" Beauville
  —9-passenger station wagon

364 Model-Color Selections

- 19 Models in Three Great Series
- 15 Modern Colors (13 NEW)
- 10 Solid Colors
- 14 Two-Tone Combinations
- NEW Two-Tone Color Styling**
- NEW *Choice* of Convertible-top Colors

Fashionable New Interiors

- NEW Striking Fabrics and Vinyls**
- NEW Seat and Sidewall Styling**
- NEW Contemporary Interiors**
- NEW Custom-Colored Interiors***

Bold New Motoramic Styling

- NEW Longer Car Length and Lines
- NEW Longer Hood; New Ornament
- NEW Smart "V" Emblems (V8)
- NEW Deeper Headlight Hoods
- NEW Full-Width Lattice Grille
- NEW Massive Bumpers and Guards
- NEW Dynamic Fender Lines
- NEW Rakish Wheel Openings
- NEW Speedline Chrome Styling**
- NEW Nameplate Locations**
- NEW Bel Air Wheel Disks
- NEW Parking and Taillight Styling
- NEW Taillight Gas Tank Filler

*—Added during 1955 Season.   **—Individual for each series.   ***—Individual for Bel Air and "Two-Ten" models.

More Powerful Engines

- 3 to 14% More Powerful "Blue-Flame 140" —New High Compression Ratio
- 5% More Powerful "Turbo-Fire V8" —When Used With Powerglide
- 14% More Powerful "Super Turbo-Fire V8"—New Ultra-High Compression ratio

And Many Other Improvements, Including:

- NEW Higher-Lift Camshafts
- Hydraulic Valve Lifters and Extra-Alloy Exhaust Valves in All Engines
- NEW Carburetor Warmup De-Icing
- NEW Full-Flow Oil Filter Option
- Heavier-Duty Clutches (V8)
- NEW More Powerful Headlights
- NEW Long-Life Battery
- IMPROVED Electrical System
- NEW Better Windshield Defrosting
- NEW Safer Rotary Door Latches
- NEW Seat Belts (Accessories)
- NEW Ashtray in "One-Fifty" Models
- Turn Signals at No Extra Cost

PLUS . . . Many NEW Accessories!

Important New Features in

THE WIDEST, MOST EXCITING
CHOICE OF MODELS IN
CHEVROLET HISTORY!

4-Door Convenience . . .
Plus the Airiness of Open Sides!

1956 CHEVROLET

THE THRILLING NEW CHEVROLET

New Styling and Colors

Whether a person is young or old, he will thrill to the exciting longer lines and gay new colors of the 1956 Chevrolet. Whether he is driver or passenger he will enjoy the good taste expressed in the smart new styling and colorful new fabrics of the car's interior. Whether he has driven one mile or a million, he will experience new driving pleasure when commanding any of Chevrolet's improved, efficient and powerful engines. And, whether he is well-to-do or of moderate means, he will be glad to know there's a car intended for him in Chevrolet's greatly expanded line.

Improved Engines

Altogether, Chevrolet provides a line of 364 model-color combinations from which to choose. Although each of these cars is inherently different from the others—because of its particular purpose, equipment, and details of appearance—it has characteristics that are common to all Chevrolets and that make every Chevrolet outstanding in value.

Common Features of All Models

With its fresh, eager, champing-at-the-bit look, every new Chevrolet stands out as an example of tasteful, modern styling. Without exaggerated massiveness and bolted-on decoration, it is *simply* beautiful. In its lovely and gracious two-tone interior, there is luxurious sitting-room comfort for all passengers, and there's plenty of room for their luggage as well. Superb vision gives an outdoor living-room effect. Ventilation is healthful and easy to control.

Appearance

Comfort

Every driving control is easy to reach; every instrument is easy to read. Riding is like riding on a cloud. A spherical-joint front suspension turns rural roads into ribbons of satin; broad-based rear springs take the edge off razor-sharp curves. There's a fine feeling of confidence and relaxation that stems from a knowledge of the car's bed-rock roadability, all-steel body protection, and the efficient stopping power of its massive brakes.

Riding

Safety

Compact design and ball-bearing steering ease simplify maneuvering in traffic and parking; the car handles with a precision that cannot be duplicated in larger cars.

Without an ounce of excess weight, the 1956 Chevrolet has more get-up-and-go; ranks among the liveliest on the road. The modern valve-in-head engine, alive with high-compression power, goes into blazing action at a touch of a toe. Acceleration is brilliant; passing is swift for safety; cruising is effortless.

Then too, every Chevrolet has all the fundamental values for which Chevrolet is famous the world over: highest quality, down-to-earth dependability, and economy of operation and upkeep that puts more miles of motoring pleasure in every dollar.

Only Chevrolet, with its enormous resources and great savings through highest volume production and mass purchasing could possibly provide a car that gives so much yet costs so little to buy and maintain.

BODIES FOR EVERY PURPOSE

Body by Fisher

Striking in every model are the fine craftsmanship and style for which Body by Fisher is famous. No other make of body is so well known for careful attention to detail and consideration for comfort; no other approaches Fisher's traditional excellence. Fisher bodies grace the finest cars on the road . . . are exclusive to Chevrolet in its field!

Chevrolet bodies by Fisher may be grouped in three classes: the conventional four-door and two-door sedan types, the sport models, and the station wagons.

The conventional sedans are all the same

Conventional Sedans

basic design, with essentially the same size passenger compartment and trunk. The *four-door sedans* provide direct access to both front and rear seats. The *two-door sedans* provide ease of entry to the front seat through extra-wide doors, while access to the rear seat is aided by front-seat backrests that tilt inward as they are folded forward. The *utility sedan* is a two-door sedan in which a luggage compartment is provided instead of a rear seat. The two-door *club coupe* provides full sedan roominess with special appointments and an all-vinyl interior.

BASIC BODY DIFFERENCES

4-DOOR MODELS

Conventional Sedan: Four doors, floor-to-top center pillars, solid-back front and rear seats, trunk with wheel well.

Sport Sedan: Four doors, no center pillars between belt and top, lower top but same rear deck as conventional sedan.

Six-Passenger Station Wagon: Four doors, endgates, folding rear seat, load platform, wheel well under platform.

Nine-Passenger Station Wagon: Four doors, endgates, middle seat consisting of two individual folding sections, rear seat consisting of removable backrest and cushion.

2-DOOR MODELS

Conventional Sedan: Extra-large doors, center pillars, same rear deck as conventional 4-door sedan, center-fold front-seat backrests, solid-back rear seat (replaced by load platform in utility sedan). (Special club coupe version.)

Sport Coupe: Extra-large doors, no center pillars between belt and top, lower top and longer rear deck than conventional sedans, center-fold front-seat backrests.

Convertible: Extra-large doors, folding top, same height and deck length as sport coupe, center-fold front-seat backrests.

Six-Passenger Station Wagon: Extra-large doors, endgates, center-fold front-seat backrests, folding rear seat, load platform, wheel well under platform. (Nomad shown.)

Among the sport models are the sport coupes and the convertible. The basic body for these models has a lower top and a longer rear deck than the conventional sedan bodies, to give the extra-long, low raciness so desired in fun cars. The *sport coupes* feature hardtop styling—the airiness of open sides with the security of a solid steel top; the *convertible* has a power-operated, folding fabric top. Otherwise these two models are like the two-door sedans in that they have extra-wide doors and center-fold front-seat backrests. In the new *sport sedans*, the newest kind of cars in the low-price field, are found all the styling and safety advantages of the two-door hardtops—plus sedan roominess and four-door convenience.

The basic body of the six-passenger station wagons features a large cargo compartment behind the two seats, a rear seat that folds level with the load platform to enlarge the compartment, a spare wheel well below the platform, tail- and liftgates in the rear, and unique wraparound rear-quarter windows. The *two-door station wagons*, like the two-door sedans, have extra-large doors and center-fold front-seat backrests. The *four-door station wagon* offers direct access to both front and rear seats and the convenience of curbside loading. The two-door *Nomad* provides the same double-duty convenience as the other six-passenger station wagons, but has an individual styling that is outstanding.

The new *nine-passenger station wagons* are identical with the six-passenger four-door station wagon except for the two rear seats. The seat behind the driver's seat is in two side-by-side units (one for one passenger; the other for two passengers) that fold individually. The rearmost seat is in two sections that make it easy to remove. An extension of the floor at the same level as for the front and middle seats provides unusual legroom for a seat of this type. A folding section of the platform covers the foot space so the full cargo platform surface is usable.

For safety, *every* Chevrolet body is of all-steel construction, *every* Chevrolet door is hinged at the front, and *every* Chevrolet window glass is high-quality safety glass.

Sport
Models

Six-
Passenger
Station
Wagons

Nine-
Passenger
Station
Wagons

Safety
Features

The new Chevrolet is offered in three series with prices scaled so anyone can choose the car he wants at a price that suits his means.

Beautiful Simplicity

From the thrifty "One-Fifty" series, one may choose a four-door sedan, two-door sedan, utility sedan, or a two-door station wagon. These are all full-size cars—practical, smart, and complete with every item needed for years of satisfying service. They feature all the new trim and crisp beauty of line that sets Chevrolets apart as the best-looking cars in their field. Adding sparkle to this beauty is the chrome of the car-wide radiator grille, hood ornament, front and rear emblems, bumpers and guards, light rims, ventipane frames, door handles, and hub caps—

"One-Fifty" Series

plus *Chevrolet* on the rear fenders. And, in addition, for the first time in cars of this class, chrome caps the rubber seals of the windshield and rear window and, in the form of sweeping moldings that terminate at rear-quarter sash moldings, decorates the body sides. Each may be had, with a new *Contemporary* interior, in a wide selection of new solid colors and *speedline* as well as conventional two-tone combinations.

Distinctive Styling

In the "Two-Ten" series, one may select from conventional and sport sedans, two-door sedan, club coupe, sport coupe, two four-door station wagons (six or nine passengers) and a two-door station wagon. Each

"Two-Ten" Series

has a smart *Contemporary* interior or may be had with a choice of *Custom-Colored* interiors. More conveniences, such as armrests and assist straps, also are provided. Outside, too, these models are distinguished by more chrome: in full moldings around the windshield and rear window, on the window sills, and on the sides in sweeping full-length moldings with sash moldings in the rear quarters. Many solid colors and two-tone color combinations, with either conventional or *speedline* color styling, are provided to suit the tastes of a color-conscious public.

nine-passenger four-door and the breath-taking Nomad. These are the glamor cars of the low-price field, with *Contemporary* or *Custom-Colored* interiors that rival the costliest in materials, appointments, and appearance. And the exteriors are enhanced by extra chrome around and between all window groups, in double side moldings, wheel disks, and in the Bel Air name and emblem on the rear fenders. An even wider choice of solid colors and *speedline* two-tones is offered.

An Array of Accessories

Dazzling Beauty

Bel Air Series

In the luxurious Bel Air series, Chevrolet provides conventional four-door and two-door sedans, sport sedan and sport coupe, convertible, and two station wagons—a new

All these models are complete in themselves and, model for model, have more conveniences than other cars in the Chevrolet field. But, for the person who wishes special conveniences or who drives under unusual operating conditions, Chevrolet also provides a full line of useful accessories and options—many of them new for 1956.

Accessories and Options

Chassis

Power Options

Every new Chevrolet has a basic chassis (frame, springs, wheels, and tires) that is designed to give the best riding comfort. But, for ease of control and performance that ranges from sparkling to spectacular, Chevrolet offers every selection of control and driving equipment that can be obtained in any car: standard steering or *power* steering, standard braking or *power* braking, and standard driving, overdrive, or *Power-*glide automatic driving (with either a Six or V8 engine) in *nine* different *power* teams.

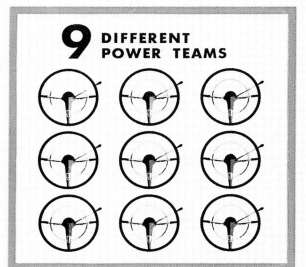

9 DIFFERENT
POWER TEAMS

16

A CAR OF HIGHEST QUALITY FOR EVERYONE

With 19 beautiful models and numerous power options including the nine different power teams, the new Chevrolet provides every practical combination of features that is available in any car—at less cost.

Best-Value Features

Chevrolet's policy is that of providing those features that assure the best value in every Chevrolet. The body types in each series are those that are most wanted by most people. The color selections and color styling for each body type are those that make it look its best. And the options and accessories for each model are those that provide the best performance, the greatest comfort, convenience and service, and the best appearance in that particular model.

Chevrolet quality exceeds that of other low-cost cars and equals that of cars that cost much more. Not only is this quality designed into the car itself but into all options and all accessories. In fact, every option and every accessory was developed as an integral part of the car with the same high standards as other Chevrolet parts.

Highest Quality

With Chevrolet's wide variety of selections, there is a model to fit nearly everyone's needs. For whatever body type a person may want, whatever styling, color, trim, or conveniences he may desire, whatever kind of performance he may prefer, the new Chevrolet provides just the right combination to suit his needs, his taste, and his budget.

A Car for Everyone

RIGID CONTROL AT EVERY STEP OF MANUFACTURE ASSURES HIGHEST QUALITY IN EVERY CHEVROLET!

CHEVROLET'S NEW ULTRA-MODERN ENGINEERING CENTER NEAR DETROIT, MICHIGAN

1956 CHEVROLET

PROGRESSIVE CHEVROLET ENGINEERING

33 Million
Chevrolets

Since Chevrolet began operating in 1911, it has produced more than 33 million vehicles which in their life spans have travelled an estimated two billion miles—equivalent to a trip around the sun and back to earth again. That these Chevrolets have performed so well that Chevrolet is famed for its economy and dependability—even in the remotest parts of the world—is a tribute to Chevrolet's progressive engineering.

Meaning
of New

The saying "There is nothing new under the sun" is only partly true in motor car design. For instance, the wheel was invented before history began but, compared to a wooden chariot wheel, the modern steel wheel of an automobile, with its tubeless pneumatic tire, *is new*. Starting with the chariot wheel, improvements added on improvements have resulted in a unit that is still a wheel but bears little resemblance to its predecessor. So it is with the Chevrolet car.

Build-Up
of Design

Today, it is impossible to guess how many minds have contributed to the design of the 1956 Chevrolet—because, since the first Chevrolet was developed, generations of talented persons have added improvements on improvements to Chevrolet design.

Chevrolet
Engineers

As a result, the 1955 Chevrolet was a record-shattering success but, since then, more than 1800 persons in Chevrolet's modern engineering offices, drafting rooms, and laboratories, and in its section of General Motors' great proving ground organization, have added their contributions to make the 1956 Chevrolet an even finer, even more enjoyable, and even better performing car. Countless engineers, stylists, scientists, and technicians, from other General Motors organizations and from Chevrolet's hundreds of sources of supply, also gave liberally of their knowledge and skills to make the 1956 model the best Chevrolet ever developed.

Other
Contributors

GM Proving Ground, Phoenix, Arizona

GM Proving Ground, Milford, Michigan

To guide these persons in their work toward a common goal, Chevrolet's code of ethics is always kept in mind.

CHEVROLET ENGINEERING CODE

Our first responsibility is to the customer. This explains our maxim "progress through constant improvement." By progress, we do not mean that we grasp at every new or radical idea but, on the contrary, that we advance by means of fundamental improvements in design. We do not believe in trying out new ideas on the customer. Instead, we adhere to the policy of providing the customer with only the best of designs that we have proved to be sound through exhaustive tests. To give Chevrolet customers ever better values, we do everything in our power to protect Chevrolet's position in the low-price field. Through unbiased tests of competitors' products, we keep posted on their designs, so that we know how to make ours even better. Our favorite policy is self-criticism. Before a new model goes into production, we do everything we can to find fault with it . . . so the customer will find it faultless. Above all, at no time do we compromise with safety in the Chevrolet!

1956 CHEVROLET

Torture-testing a Chevrolet on the Belgian Block Road at the GM Proving Ground, Milford, Michigan.

SOME FAMOUS FIRSTS OF THE LOW-PRICE FIELD!

(Features of modern cars introduced by Chevrolet before both Ford and Plymouth.)

1914 Valve-in-Head Engine ● Three-Speed Transmission ● Electric Lights ● Oil Pump ● Accelerator ● Speedometer **1915** Electric Starter ● Storage Battery Ignition ● Instrument Panel ● Oil-Pressure Indicator . . . **WORLD WAR I** . . . **1919** Water Pump ● V-Belt **1923** Body by Fisher ● Rear Gas Tank ● Semi-Floating Axle **1924** Window Cranks **1925** Lacquer Finish ● Automatic Windshield Wiper ● Semi-Elliptic Springs **1927** Remote Door Controls ● Air Cleaner **1928** Indirect Instrument Lighting ● Cooling System Thermostat **1929** Six-Cylinder Engine ● Scientific Crankshaft Balancing ● Fuel Pump ● Crankcase Ventilation ● Heat Indicator ● Headlight Foot Switch ● Adjustable Rearview Mirror **1930** Gas Gauge **1931** Harmonic Balancer **1932** Downdraft Carburetor ● Counter-balanced Crankshaft ● Stabilized Front-End ● Radiator Grille ● Sunshades **1933** Ventipanes ● Fender Skirts ● Trunk ● Button-on-Sill Locks ● Automatic Manifold Heat Control ● Dual Automatic Spark Control ● Octane Selector ● Flanged Axle Shafts **1934** Knee-Action ● Double-Acting Shock Absorbers ● Wedge Combustion Chambers ● Ventipane Cranks ● Glove Compartment with Key Lock **1935** Turret Top ● Complete Body Insulation ● Spare Wheel in Trunk ● Tin-Plated Pistons

1936 Box-Girder Frame ● Doorpull Armrests **1937** Unisteel Body ● Inclined-Plane Seat Adjustment **1938** Diaphragm-Spring Clutch ● Positive-Shift Starter **1940** Keyless Door Locking ● Instrument Light Control ● Glove Compartment Light **1941** Front-Hinged Doors ● Key Locks on Both Sides ● Automatic Domelight Switches ● Two-Tone Exteriors . . . **WORLD WAR II** . . . **1948** Single Car Key **1949** Foam-Rubber Cushions ● Windshield-Wide Defrosting ● Pushbutton Door Handles ● Key-Release Trunk Lid ● Bonded Brake Linings ● **1950** Hardtop Body Styling ● Wrap-around Rear Window ● Automatic Transmission ● Hydraulic Valve Lifters **1953** Hydraulic Power Steering **1954** Built-In Armrests ● Power-Positioned Seat ● Power-Controlled Windows ● Power Brakes **1955** High-Level Ventilation ● Panoramic Windshield ● Four-Fender Visibility ● Integral Headlight Hoods ● Dipdown Belt Line ● Air Conditioner ● Spherical-Joint Suspension ● Outrigger Rear Suspension ● Anti-Dive Braking ● 12-Volt Electrical System ● Dual Exhaust System ● Ball-Race Steering **1956** Precision-Aimed Headlights ● Long-Life Battery.

1956 CHEVROLET

As a result of this code, with every new model Chevrolet has taken a firm step forward in motor car design, providing the customer with better appearance, better performance, better handling and riding qualities, greater convenience and safety, more room for greater comfort, and greater durability that in Chevrolet's history has increased the life expectancy of the car from 25,000 miles to an estimated 125,000 miles.

As a result of this code also, Chevrolet has consistently led its field in introducing the finest features first—features which are fundamentally sound so that they remain as modern tomorrow as they are today. These Chevrolet *firsts* embrace every phase of motor car design and together have raised the field's standards so high that every customer benefits substantially—not only every Chevrolet customer but also the customers of competitive makers who copy Chevrolet design. Outstanding among the hundreds of Chevrolet *firsts* are those that are listed on the opposite page.

Of equal importance to selecting and perfecting those features that give best satisfaction to the customer, is the determination of a car's proportions—not only in size but also in weight and power. In this respect noteworthy advances have been made in the Chevrolet—advances that can only be appreciated by a study of the car's specifications over a period of years.

The chart on the next two pages shows such specifications for the past ten years. In this one decade, the car weight has been increased 200 pounds, because of extra values built into the car—and horsepower has been more than doubled. For handling ease, the length has not been increased, yet there are about three inches more legroom for *each* seat. Width is only one inch greater, yet the front seat is 3½ inches broader and the rear seat is fully 13½ inches wider. And, for better appearance and a lower center of gravity, car height has been reduced 5½ inches—with the same road clearance and with headroom equal to that of the most expensive cars.

Design Progress

Chevrolet Firsts

Size and Power Advances

Postwar Progress

More Power . . . for better, safer performance. Lower Height . . . for lower, safer center of gravity. More Vision Area . . . for better, safer vision. More Room . . . for better, safer driving comfort.

	1946-48	1949	1950	1951
	Sportmaster Sedan 6-Cylinder Engine Synchro-Mesh	Styleline Sedan 6-Cylinder Engine Synchro-Mesh	Styleline Sedan 6-Cylinder Engine Powerglide	Styleline Sedan 6-Cylinder Engine Powerglide
Dry Weight (lb.)	3150	3125	3280	3280
Horsepower	90	90	105	105
Pounds per Horsepower	35.0	34.7	31.2	31.2
Brake Diameter (in.)	11.0	11.0	11.0	11.0
Length (in.)	197.8	196.9	197.5	197.8
Width (in.)	73.4	73.9	73.9	73.9
Height (in.)	66.1	63.6	63.6	63.6
Wheelbase (in.)	116.0	115.0	115.0	115.0
Front Tread (in.)	57.6	57.0	56.6	56.7
Rear Tread (in.)	60.0	58.8	58.8	58.8
Rear Spring Centers (in.)	48.0	45.3	45.3	45.3
Turning Diameter (ft.)	41.0	39.5	38.0	38.0
Front Ramp Angle (degrees)	22	26	26	26
Rear Ramp Angle (degrees)	16	14	14	14
Road Clearance (in.)	7.8	8.1	8.1	8.0
Front Seat Headroom (in.)	37.5	35.4	35.4	35.4
Front Seat Legroom (in.)	41.0	42.8	42.8	42.8
Front Seat Hiproom (in.)	58.3	60.0	60.0	60.0
Front Seat Shoulder Room (in.)	54.8	54.6	54.3	54.3
Rear Seat Headroom (in.)	35.8	35.0	35.0	35.0
Rear Seat Legroom (in.)	39.0	41.0	41.0	41.0
Rear Seat Hiproom (in.)	49.4	58.4	59.0	59.0
Rear Seat Shoulder Room (in.)	54.3	53.8	52.5	53.9
Vision Area (sq. ft.)	14.7	19.1	19.1	19.1
Trunk Space (cu. ft.)	17.0	19.0	19.0	19.0

*Principal dimensions of leading four-door sedan in line, equipped with most powerful engine and most advanced transmission for each model year.

1956 CHEVROLET

1952	1953	1954	1955	1956

Styleline Sedan 6-Cylinder Engine Powerglide	Bel Air Sedan "Blue-Flame" 6 Powerglide	Bel Air Sedan "Blue-Flame" 6 Powerglide	Bel Air Sedan "Super Turbo-Fire V8" Powerglide	Bel Air Sedan "Super Turbo-Fire V8" Powerglide
3265	3365	3355	3300	3370
105	115	125	180	205
31.1	29.3	26.8	18.3	16.4
11.0	11.0	11.0	11.0	11.0
197.6	195.5	196.5	195.6	197.5
74.8	75.0	75.0	74.0	74.0
63.6	63.1	63.1	60.5	60.5
115.0	115.0	115.0	115.0	115.0
56.7	56.7	56.7	58.0	58.0
58.8	58.8	58.8	58.8	58.8
45.3	45.3	45.3	46.0	46.0
38.0	38.0	38.0	38.0	41.5
26	26	26	28	25
14	16	15	16	15
8.0	8.0	8.0	8.0	8.0
35.4	35.8	35.8	35.6	35.6
42.8	42.7	42.7	43.7	43.7
60.0	59.8	59.8	62.0	62.0
54.3	54.9	54.9	56.8	56.8
35.0	35.1	35.1	35.6	35.6
41.0	41.4	41.4	42.6	42.6
58.4	60.0	60.0	63.0	63.0
53.9	53.9	53.9	56.6	56.6
19.1	20.7	20.7	24.4	24.4
19.0	22.0	22.0	20.0	20.0

8 NEW SEDANS

SERIES	4-DOOR SEDANS	2-DOOR SEDANS	CLUB COUPE	UTILITY SEDAN
BEL AIR	Model 2403 Page 28	Model 2402 Page 34		
"TWO-TEN"	Model 2103 Page 30	Model 2102 Page 36	Model 2124 Page 38	
"ONE-FIFTY"	Model 1503 Page 32	Model 1502 Page 40		Model 1512 Page 42

IN 3 GREAT SERIES

5 NEW SPORT MODELS			6 NEW STATION WAGONS		
4-DOOR SPORT SEDAN	SPORT COUPE	CONVERTIBLE	4-DOOR 9-PASSENGER	4-DOOR 6-PASSENGER	2-DOOR 6-PASSENGER
Model 2413 Page 44	Model 2454 Page 48	Model 2434 Page 52	Model 2419 Page 54		Model 2429 Page 60
Model 2113 Page 46	Model 2154 Page 50		Model 2119 Page 56	Model 2109 Page 58	Model 2129 Page 62
					Model 1529 Page 64

CAR SIZE

Overall length	197.5" (16.5 ft.)
Overall width	74.0" (6.2 ft.)
Loaded height	60.5" (5.0 ft.)
Wheelbase	115.0" (9.6 ft.)
Wheel tread (av)	58.4" (4.9 ft.)
Ramp angles	Front 25°, Rear 15°
Road clearance, loaded	8.0"

POWER AND WEIGHT

POWER TEAM	140-hp SIX	170-hp V8*	205-hp V8
Synchro-Mesh	3235 lb.	3205 lb.	3240 lb.
Overdrive	3265 lb.	3235 lb.	3270 lb.
Powerglide	3335 lb.	3305 lb.	3340 lb.

Add 130 lb. for gas and water, 150 for each
passenger.

*162-hp with Synchro-Mesh or Overdrive

MODELS

DISTINGUISHING FEATURES

Two of every five buyers select a four-door sedan . . . and here is the leading four-door in its field. Ten solid color selections; 13 two-tones with Speedline color styling. Charcoal-and-ivory Contemporary interior; optional Custom-Colored interiors.

All-steel body with four doors and large trunk. Rear-door safety locks. Crank-operated door windows and ventipanes; extra rear-quarter windows. High-quality safety glass.

Foam-rubber-cushioned seats for six. Cushions and backrests upholstered in *jacquard-type* pattern cloth that looks like striated plywood; vinyl bolsters and facings. All-vinyl sidewalls. Deep-pile carpets.

Three-spoke steering wheel, horn ring, two windshield wipers and sunshades, lighted lockable glove compartment, electric clock, cigaret lighter, ashtrays and built-in door-pull armrests front and rear, two coat hooks, parcel shelf, and a central domelight with an automatic switch at each door.

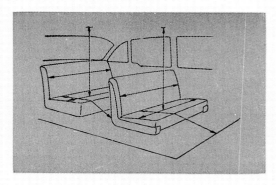

ROOMINESS	Rear	Front
Headroom	35.1"	35.6"
Shoulder room	56.6"	56.8"
Hiproom	63.0"	62.0"
Legroom	42.6"	43.7"
Total seat adjustment		4.4"

VISION AREA . . . . 24.4 sq. ft.

TRUNK CAPACITY . . . . 20.0 cu. ft.

CAR SIZE

Overall length . . . . 197.5" (16.5 ft.)
Overall width . . . . 74.0" (6.2 ft.)
Loaded height . . . . 60.5" (5.0 ft.)
Wheelbase . . . . 115.0" (9.6 ft.)
Wheel tread (av) . . . . 58.4" (4.9 ft.)
Ramp angles . . . . Front 25°, Rear 15°
Road clearance, loaded . . . . 8.0"

POWER AND WEIGHT

POWER TEAM	140-hp SIX	170-hp V8*	205-hp V8
Synchro-Mesh	3220 lb.	3190 lb.	3225 lb.
Overdrive	3250 lb.	3220 lb.	3255 lb.
Powerglide	3320 lb.	3290 lb.	3325 lb.

Add 130 lb. for gas and water, 150 for each passenger.

*162-hp with Synchro-mesh or Overdrive

MODELS

DISTINGUISHING FEATURES

The favorite six-passenger family car. A choice of ten solid colors, and 12 two-tones with conventional or Speedline color styling. Charcoal-and-ivory Contemporary interior; optional Custom-Colored interiors.

All-steel body with four doors and roomy trunk; rear-door safety locks. Crank-operated door windows and ventipanes; extra rear-quarter windows. High-quality safety glass in all windows.

Foam-rubber-cushioned front seat. Horizontally ribbed pattern cloth on seats, with vinyl bolsters and facings. All-vinyl sidewalls. Vinyl-coated rubber floor mats. Rubber mat on floor of trunk.

Two-spoke steering wheel, horn ring, two windshield wipers, two sunshades, lighted lockable glove compartment, cigaret lighter, ashtrays and applied door-pull armrests in front and rear, two coat hooks, parcel shelf, and a central domelight with automatic switches at both front doors.

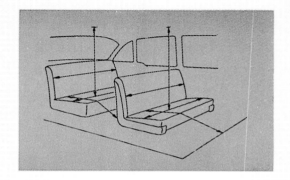

ROOMINESS	Rear	Front
Headroom	35.1"	35.6"
Shoulder room	56.6"	56.8"
Hiproom	63.0"	62.0"
Legroom	42.6"	43.7"
Total seat adjustment		4.4"

VISION AREA .... 24.4 sq. ft.

TRUNK CAPACITY .... 20.0 cu. ft

CAR SIZE

Overall length..................197.5″ (16.5 ft.)
Overall width..................74.0″ (6.2 ft.)
Loaded height..................60.5″ (5.0 ft.)
Wheelbase.....................115.0″ (9.6 ft.)
Wheel tread (av)...............58.4″ (4.9 ft.)
Ramp angles................Front 25°, Rear 15°
Road clearance, loaded....................8.0″

POWER AND WEIGHT

POWER TEAM	140-hp SIX	170-hp V8*	205-hp V8
Synchro-Mesh......	3195 lb.	3165 lb.	3200 lb.
Overdrive........	3225 lb.	3195 lb.	3230 lb.
Powerglide.......	3295 lb.	3265 lb.	3300 lb.

Add 130 lb. for gas and water, 150 for each passenger.
*162-hp with Synchro-Mesh or Overdrive

DISTINGUISHING FEATURES

An exceptional value for a full-size six-passenger car. Available in a choice of eight solid colors and six two-tones in either conventional or Speedline color styling. Gold-and-black Contemporary interior.

All-steel body with four doors and roomy trunk; key locks for both front doors, rear-door safety locks. Crank-operated windows and ventipanes; extra rear-quarter windows. High-quality safety glass all around.

Cushions and backrests upholstered in a rich pattern cloth which features small two-tone triangles offset by gold flecks. Bolsters of gold ribbed-vinyl; plain gold vinyl on seat facings. All-vinyl sidewalls repeat seat trim in color and appearance. Gold cloth headlining; black rubber floor mats.

Two-spoke steering wheel with horn button, two windshield wipers, sunshade, instrument panel ashtray, lockable glove compartment, parcel shelf, and central domelight.

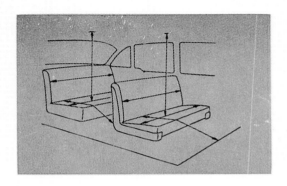

ROOMINESS	Rear	Front
Headroom	35.1"	35.6"
Shoulder room	56.6"	56.8"
Hiproom	63.0"	62.0"
Legroom	42.6"	43.7"
Total seat adjustment		4.4"

VISION AREA . . . . 24.4 sq. ft.

TRUNK CAPACITY . . . . 20.0 cu. ft.

CAR SIZE

Overall length . . . . 197.5" (16.5 ft.)
Overall width . . . . 74.0" (6.2 ft.)
Loaded height . . . . 60.5" (5.0 ft.)
Wheelbase . . . . 115.0" (9.6 ft.)
Wheel tread (av) . . . . 58.4" (4.9 ft.)
Ramp angles . . . . Front 25°, Rear 15°
Road clearance, loaded . . . . 8.0"

POWER AND WEIGHT

POWER TEAM	140-hp SIX	170-hp V8*	205-hp V8
Synchro-Mesh	3195 lb.	3165 lb.	3200 lb.
Overdrive	3225 lb.	3195 lb.	3230 lb.
Powerglide	3295 lb.	3265 lb.	3300 lb.

Add 130 lb. for gas and water, 150 for each passenger.
*162-hp with Synchro-Mesh or Overdrive

DISTINGUISHING FEATURES

Three of every ten buyers favor two-door sedans because of their convenience and smart appearance. Available in ten solid colors and 13 two-tones with Speedline color styling. Charcoal-and-ivory Contemporary interior; optional Custom-Colored interiors.

All-steel six-passenger body with large doors and trunk. Crank-operated ventipanes and side windows. High-quality safety glass.

Foam-rubber-cushioned seats; center-fold front-seat backrests. Cushions and backrests upholstered in *jacquard-type* pattern cloth resembling striated plywood in appearance. All-vinyl sidewalls. Deep-pile carpets.

Three-spoke steering wheel, horn ring, two windshield wipers, two sunshades, lighted lockable glove compartment, electric clock, cigaret lighter, ashtrays in front and rear, built-in front armrests, applied rear armrests, assist straps, coat hooks, parcel shelf, domelight with automatic door switches.

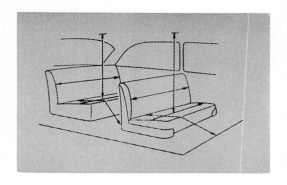

ROOMINESS	Rear	Front
Headroom	35.1"	35.6"
Shoulder room	56.6"	56.8"
Hiproom	63.0"	62.0"
Legroom	42.6"	43.7"
Total seat adjustment		4.4"

VISION AREA . . . . 24.7 sq. ft.

TRUNK CAPACITY . . . . 20.0 cu. ft.

CAR SIZE

Overall length	197.5" (16.5 ft.)
Overall width	74.0" (6.2 ft.)
Loaded height	60.5" (5.0 ft.)
Wheelbase	115.0" (9.6 ft.)
Wheel tread (av)	58.4" (4.9 ft.)
Ramp angles	Front 25°, Rear 15°
Road clearance, loaded	8.0"

POWER AND WEIGHT

POWER TEAM	140-hp SIX	170-hp V8*	205-hp V8
Synchro-Mesh	3185 lb.	3155 lb.	3190 lb.
Overdrive	3215 lb.	3185 lb.	3220 lb.
Powerglide	3285 lb.	3255 lb.	3290 lb.

Add 130 lb. for gas and water, 150 for each passenger.

*162-hp with Synchro-Mesh or Overdrive

DISTINGUISHING FEATURES

Parents with small children often prefer a two-door sedan. This six-passenger car is available in ten solid colors and 12 two-tones (conventional or Speedline color styling). Charcoal-and-ivory Contemporary interior; optional Custom-Colored interiors.

All-steel body with extra-large doors and roomy trunk. Crank-operated windows and ventipanes. High-quality safety glass.

Foam-rubber-cushioned front seat with center-fold backrest. Horizontally ribbed pattern cloth on seats, with all-vinyl bolsters and facings. All-vinyl sidewalls. Vinyl-coated rubber floor mats. Rubber trunk mat.

Two-spoke steering wheel with horn ring, two windshield wipers, two sunshades, lighted lockable glove compartment, cigaret lighter, ashtrays front and rear, applied-type armrests for both seats, assist straps, coat hooks, parcel shelf, and a central domelight with automatic switches at both doors.

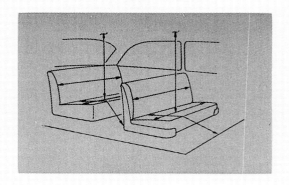

ROOMINESS	Rear	Front
Headroom	35.1"	35.6"
Shoulder room	56.6"	56.8"
Hiproom	63.0"	62.0"
Legroom	42.6"	43.7"
Total seat adjustment		4.4"

VISION AREA .... 24.7 sq. ft.

TRUNK CAPACITY .... 20.0 cu. ft.

CAR SIZE

Overall length . . . . 197.5" (16.5 ft.)
Overall width . . . . 74.0" (6.2 ft.)
Loaded height . . . . 60.5" (5.0 ft.)
Wheelbase . . . . 115.0" (9.6 ft.)
Wheel tread (av) . . . . 58.4" (4.9 ft.)
Ramp angles . . . . Front 25°, Rear 15°
Road clearance, loaded . . . . 8.0"

POWER AND WEIGHT

POWER TEAM	140-hp SIX	170-hp V8*	205-hp V8
Synchro-Mesh	3185 lb.	3155 lb.	3190 lb.
Overdrive	3215 lb.	3185 lb.	3220 lb.
Powerglide	3285 lb.	3255 lb.	3290 lb.

Add 130 lb. for gas and water, 150 for each passenger.

*162-hp with Synchro-Mesh or Overdrive

DISTINGUISHING FEATURES

A smart six-passenger car with full sedan roominess and a washable, durable all-vinyl interior that's made for family use. Nine solid color selections; ten two-tones with conventional or Speedline color styling. Ivory - and - black Contemporary interior; optional Custom-Colored interiors.

All-steel body with extra-large doors and big trunk. Crank-operated windows and ventipanes. High-quality safety glass.

Foam-rubber-cushioned front seat with center-fold backrests. Cushions and back-rests garnished by stitching that forms rectangular panels. Perforated vinyl headlining. Deep-pile carpets. Rubber trunk mat.

Two-spoke steering wheel with horn ring, two windshield wipers, two sunshades, lighted lockable glove compartment, cigaret lighter, ashtrays and armrests in front and rear, assist straps, coat hooks, parcel shelf, and domelight with automatic door switches.

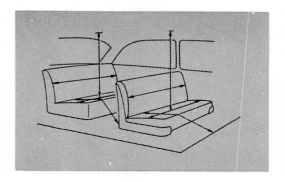

ROOMINESS	Rear	Front
Headroom	35.1″	35.6″
Shoulder room	56.6″	56.8″
Hiproom	63.0″	62.0″
Legroom	42.6″	43.7″
Total seat adjustment		4.4″

VISION AREA .... 24.7 sq. ft.

TRUNK CAPACITY .... 20.0 cu. ft.

CAR SIZE

Overall length	197.5" (16.5 ft.)
Overall width	74.0" (6.2 ft.)
Loaded height	60.5" (5.0 ft.)
Wheelbase	115.0" (9.6 ft.)
Wheel tread (av)	58.4" (4.9 ft.)
Ramp angles	Front 25°, Rear 15°
Road clearance, loaded	8.0"

POWER AND WEIGHT

POWER TEAM	140-hp SIX	170-hp V8*	205-hp V8
Synchro-Mesh	3155 lb.	3125 lb.	3160 lb.
Overdrive	3185 lb.	3155 lb.	3190 lb.
Powerglide	3255 lb.	3225 lb.	3260 lb.

Add 130 lb. for gas and water, 150 for each passenger.

*162-hp with Synchro-Mesh or Overdrive

DISTINGUISHING FEATURES

A good-looking, practical six-passenger model at low cost. Eight solid color selections; plus six two-tones, in either conventional or Speedline color styling. Smart gold-and-black Contemporary interior.

All-steel body with extra-large doors and spacious trunk. Crank-operated windows and ventipanes. High-quality safety glass.

Center-fold front-seat backrests. Cushions and backrests upholstered in a rich pattern cloth. All-vinyl sidewalls that repeat the seat trim in color and appearance, with gold ribbed upper panels and scuff pads, and center panels that simulate the pattern cloth. Gold headlining; black rubber floor mats.

Two-spoke steering wheel with large horn button, two windshield wipers, a sunshade for the driver, instrument panel ashtray, lockable glove compartment, parcel shelf, and central domelight controlled by light switch on instrument panel.

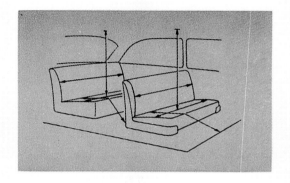

ROOMINESS	Rear	Front
Headroom	35.1"	35.6"
Shoulder room	56.6"	56.8"
Hiproom	63.0"	62.0"
Legroom	42.6"	43.7"
Total seat adjustment		4.4"

VISION AREA .... 24.7 sq. ft.

TRUNK CAPACITY .... 20.0 cu. ft.

CAR SIZE

Overall length	197.5" (16.5 ft.)
Overall width	74.0" (6.2 ft.)
Loaded height	60.5" (5.0 ft.)
Wheelbase	115.0" (9.6 ft.)
Wheel tread (av)	58.4" (4.9 ft.)
Ramp angles	Front 25°, Rear 15°
Road clearance, loaded	8.0"

POWER AND WEIGHT

POWER TEAM	140-hp SIX	170-hp V8*	205-hp V8
Synchro-Mesh	3120 lb.	3090 lb.	3125 lb.
Overdrive	3150 lb.	3120 lb.	3155 lb.
Powerglide	3220 lb.	3190 lb.	3225 lb.

Add 130 lb. for gas and water, 150 for each passenger.

*162-hp with Synchro-Mesh or Overdrive

MODELS

DISTINGUISHING FEATURES

This car means *business*. With 51 cubic feet of stowage space, it's a practical and thrifty car for the businessman who needs extra carrying capacity. Available in eight solid colors and six two-tones, in either conventional or Speedline color styling. Smart gold-and-black Contemporary interior.

All-steel body with extra-large doors, roomy trunk, and big load compartment with flat platform. Black rubber floor mats. Crank-operated door windows and ventipanes. High-quality safety glass. Durable composition-board loadspace walls.

Three-passenger seat, with center-fold backrests, upholstered in a rich pattern cloth: gold vinyl seat facings.

Two-spoke steering wheel with horn button, two windshield wipers, sunshade for driver, instrument panel ashtray, lockable glove compartment, parcel shelf, central domelight operated by main light switch.

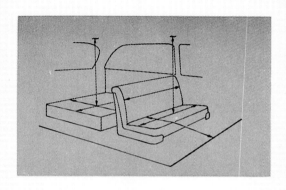

SEAT ROOM

Headroom.....35.6"		Shoulder room...56.8"
Legroom.......43.7"		Hiproom.......62.0"
Total adjustment.....................4.4"		

LOAD COMPARTMENT

Height..........43.7" to top, 23.0" to window sills
Length and width at floor...........36.4" x 61.0"
Capacity..............31 cu. ft. (trunk 20 cu. ft.)

VISION AREA.......................24.6 sq. ft.

CAR SIZE

Overall length	197.5" (16.5 ft.)
Overall width	74.0" (6.2 ft.)
Loaded height	59.1" (4.9 ft.)
Wheelbase	115.0" (9.6 ft.)
Wheel tread (av)	58.4" (4.9 ft.)
Ramp angles	Front 25°, Rear 15°
Road clearance, loaded	8.0"

POWER AND WEIGHT

POWER TEAM	140-hp SIX	170-hp V8*	205-hp V8
Synchro-Mesh	3290 lb.	3260 lb.	3295 lb.
Overdrive	3320 lb.	3290 lb.	3325 lb.
Powerglide	3390 lb.	3360 lb.	3395 lb.

Add 130 lb. for gas and water, 150 for each passenger.

*162-hp with Synchro-Mesh or Overdrive

44

DISTINGUISHING FEATURES

A beautiful new honey of a hardtop—with open sides, steel-top protection, and four-door convenience. In a choice of ten solid colors and 13 two-tones with Speedline color styling. Ivory-and-charcoal Contemporary interior; optional Custom-Colored interiors.

All-steel body with reinforced hinge pillars; spacious trunk. Crank-operated ventipanes and windows. High-quality safety glass.

Foam - rubber - cushioned seats for six. Cushions and backrests upholstered in distinctive *jaquard* bark-pattern cloth. Vinyl cushion and backrest bolsters and cushion facings. Perforated vinyl headlining; vinyl sidewalls. Deep-pile carpets.

Three-spoke steering wheel, horn ring, windshield wipers, sunshades, lighted lockable glove compartment, electric clock, cigaret lighter, ashtrays and built-in armrests front and rear, parcel shelf, coat hooks, automatic domelight switches at all doors.

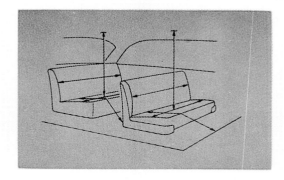

ROOMINESS	Rear	Front
Headroom	33.6″	34.0″
Shoulder room	56.8″	56.0″
Hiproom	62.9″	61.7″
Legroom	41.8″	43.5″
Total seat adjustment		4.4″

VISION AREA	22.9 sq. ft.
TRUNK CAPACITY	20.0 cu. ft.

MODELS

CAR SIZE

Overall length	197.5" (16.5 ft.)
Overall width	74.0" (6.2 ft.)
Loaded height	59.1" (4.9 ft.)
Wheelbase	115.0" (9.6 ft.)
Wheel tread (av)	58.4" (4.9 ft.)
Ramp angles	Front 25°, Rear 15°
Road clearance, loaded	8.0"

POWER AND WEIGHT

POWER TEAM	140-hp SIX	170-hp V8*	205-hp V8
Synchro-Mesh	3285 lb.	3255 lb.	3290 lb.
Overdrive	3315 lb.	3285 lb.	3320 lb.
Powerglide	3385 lb.	3355 lb.	3390 lb.

Add 130 lb. for gas and water, 150 for each passenger.

*162-hp with Synchro-Mesh or Overdrive

Sell your books at
sellbackyourBook.com!
Go to sellbackyourBook.com
and get an instant price
quote. We even pay the
shipping - see what your old
books are worth today!

Inspected By: reyna_serrano

00044466430

0004446

6430 S

"TWO-TEN" SPORT SEDAN

DISTINGUISHING FEATURES

With its low silhouette, four-door convenience, and no center posts, this brand-new hardtop is outstanding. Ten solid color selections; 12 two-tones with conventional or Speedline color styling. Ivory-and-charcoal Contemporary interior; optional Custom-Colored interiors.

All-steel body with big trunk; reinforced door pillars. Crank-operated windows and ventipanes. High-quality safety glass.

Six-passenger capacity. Foam-rubber-cushioned front seat. Ribbed pattern cloth seat upholstery with vinyl bolsters and facings. All-vinyl sidewalls; cloth headlining. Vinyl-coated rubber floor mats.

Two-spoke steering wheel, horn ring, windshield wipers, sunshades, lighted lockable glove compartment, cigaret lighter, ashtrays and applied door-pull armrests in front and rear, parcel shelf, coat hooks, automatic domelight switches at front doors.

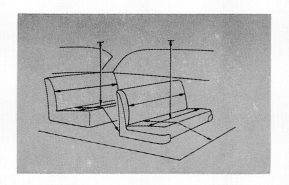

ROOMINESS	Rear	Front
Headroom	33.6"	34.0"
Shoulder room	56.8"	56.0"
Hiproom	62.9"	61.7"
Legroom	41.8"	43.5"
Total seat adjustment		4.4"

VISION AREA	22.9 sq. ft.
TRUNK CAPACITY	20.0 cu. ft.

CAR SIZE

Overall length	197.5" (16.5 ft.)
Overall width	74.0" (6.2 ft.)
Loaded height	59.1" (4.9 ft.)
Wheelbase	115.0" (9.6 ft.)
Wheel tread (av)	58.4" (4.9 ft.)
Ramp angles	Front 25°, Rear 15°
Road clearance, loaded	8.0"

POWER AND WEIGHT

POWER TEAM	140-hp SIX	170-hp V8*	205-hp V8
Synchro-Mesh	3225 lb.	3195 lb.	3230 lb.
Overdrive	3255 lb.	3225 lb.	3260 lb.
Powerglide	3325 lb.	3295 lb.	3330 lb.

Add 130 lb. for gas and water, 150 for each passenger.

*162-hp with Synchro-Mesh or Overdrive

MODELS

DISTINGUISHING FEATURES

The original style pacesetter of its field. Admired by all, it comes in ten solid colors and 13 two-tones with Speedline color styling. Charcoal-and-ivory Contemporary interior; optional Custom-Colored interiors.

All-steel hardtop body with large doors and roomy trunk. Crank-operated windows and ventipanes. High quality safety glass.

Foam-rubber-cushioned seats for six. Cushions and backrests upholstered in *jacquard* bark-pattern cloth trimmed with bright vinyl welts; vinyl backrest bolsters, cushion bolsters and facings. All-vinyl sidewalls and attractive perforated vinyl headlining. Deep-pile carpets.

Three-spoke steering wheel with horn ring, two windshield wipers, two sunshades, lighted lockable glove compartment, electric clock, cigaret lighter, ashtrays and built-in armrests front and rear, parcel shelf, coat hooks, and a central domelight with automatic switches at both doors.

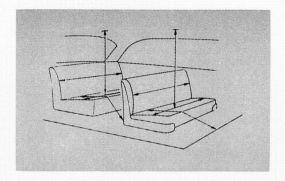

ROOMINESS	Rear	Front
Headroom	33.9"	34.4"
Shoulder room	56.7"	56.8"
Hiproom	54.2"	61.7"
Legroom	38.5"	43.4"
Total seat adjustment		4.4"

VISION AREA	23.1 sq. ft.
TRUNK CAPACITY	20.0 cu. ft.

CAR SIZE

Overall length	197.5" (16.5 ft.)
Overall width	74.0" (6.2 ft.)
Loaded height	59.1" (4.9 ft.)
Wheelbase	115.0" (9.6 ft.)
Wheel tread (av)	58.4" (4.9 ft.)
Ramp angles	Front 25°, Rear 15°
Road clearance, loaded	8.0"

POWER AND WEIGHT

POWER TEAM	140-hp SIX	170-hp V8*	205-hp V8
Synchro-Mesh	3225 lb.	3195 lb.	3230 lb.
Overdrive	3255 lb.	3225 lb.	3260 lb.
Powerglide	3325 lb.	3295 lb.	3330 lb.

Add 130 lb. for gas and water, 150 for each passenger.

*162-hp with Synchro-Mesh or Overdrive

MODELS

DISTINGUISHING FEATURES

Juniors and seniors alike enjoy the admiring glances given to this recent gay addition to the Chevrolet family. Available in ten solid colors, and 12 two-tones with conventional or Speedline color styling. Charcoal-and-ivory Contemporary interior; optional Custom-Colored interiors.

All-steel hardtop body with large doors and trunk. Crank-operated windows and ventipanes. High-quality safety glass.

Six-passenger capacity. Foam-rubber-cushioned front seat. Horizontally ribbed pattern cloth on seats, with vinyl bolsters and facings. Vinyl sidewalls; cloth headlining. Vinyl-coated rubber floor mats.

Two-spoke steering wheel with horn ring, two windshield wipers, two sunshades, lighted lockable glove compartment, cigaret lighter, ashtrays and armrests front and rear, parcel shelf, coat hooks, and a central dome-light with automatic switches at both doors.

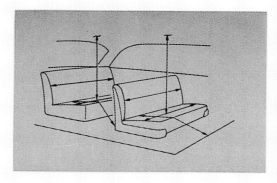

ROOMINESS	Rear	Front
Headroom	33.9"	34.4"
Shoulder room	56.7"	56.8"
Hiproom	54.2"	61.7"
Legroom	38.5"	43.4"
Total seat adjustment		4.4"

VISION AREA .... 23.1 sq. ft.

TRUNK CAPACITY .... 20.0 cu. ft.

CAR SIZE

Overall length	197.5" (16.5 ft.)
Overall width	74.0" (6.2 ft.)
Loaded height	59.1" (4.9 ft.)
Wheelbase	115.0" (9.6 ft.)
Wheel tread (av)	58.4" (4.9 ft.)
Ramp angles	Front 25°, Rear 15°
Road clearance, loaded	8.0"

POWER AND WEIGHT

POWER TEAM	140-hp SIX	170-hp V8*	205-hp V8
Synchro-Mesh	3350 lb.	3320 lb.	3355 lb.
Overdrive	3380 lb.	3350 lb.	3385 lb.
Powerglide	3450 lb.	3420 lb.	3455 lb.

Add 130 lb. for gas and water, 150 for each passenger.

*162-hp with Synchro-Mesh or Overdrive

DISTINGUISHING FEATURES

A fresh-air dream car—designed for *fun* in the large economy size. Choice of ten solid colors and 12 two-tones with Speedline color styling—each with a choice of striking top colors. Charcoal-and-ivory Contemporary interior; optional Custom-Colored interiors.

Reinforced body with roomy trunk. Hydraulically operated chevrolon top with zippered-in plastic rear window. Vinyl boot. Crank-operated ventipanes and windows. High-quality safety glass. Chrome molding inside windshield.

Foam-rubber-cushioned seats; center-fold front-seat backrests. Cushions and backrests in patterned vinyl; saddle-stitched bolsters. All-vinyl sidewalls. Deep-pile carpets.

Three-spoke steering wheel, horn ring, two windshield wipers, two sunshades, lighted lockable glove compartment, electric clock, cigaret lighter, ashtrays and built-in armrests front and rear, and two courtesy lights with automatic door switches.

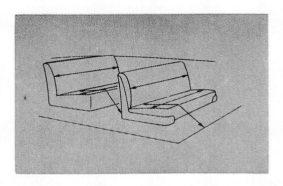

ROOMINESS	Rear	Front
Headroom	34.0"	34.2"
Shoulder room	48.4"	56.8"
Hiproom	50.1"	61.7"
Legroom	38.7"	43.4"
Total seat adjustment		4.4"

VISION AREA . . . . 19.7 sq. ft.

TRUNK CAPACITY . . . . 17.0 cu. ft.

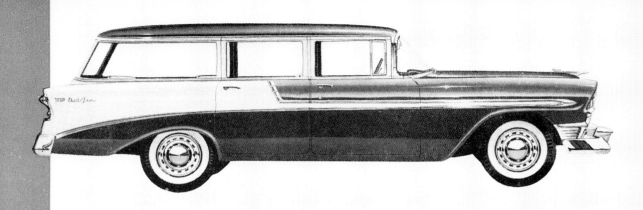

CAR SIZE

Overall length	200.8" (16.7 ft.)
Overall width	74.0" (6.2 ft.)
Loaded height	60.8" (5.1 ft.)
Wheelbase	115.0" (9.6 ft.)
Wheel tread (av)	58.4" (4.9 ft.)
Ramp angles	Front 25°, Rear 15°
Road clearance, loaded	8.0"

POWER AND WEIGHT

POWER TEAM	140-hp SIX	170-hp V8*	205-hp V8
Synchro-Mesh	3475 lb.	3445 lb.	3480 lb.
Overdrive	3505 lb.	3475 lb.	3510 lb.
Powerglide	3575 lb.	3545 lb.	3580 lb.

Add 130 lb. for gas and water, 150 for each passenger.

*162-hp with Synchro-Mesh or Overdrive

DISTINGUISHING FEATURES

Beautiful, roomy, remarkably useful . . . and brand new. Eight solid colors; ten two-tones with Speedline color styling. Charcoal-and-ivory Contemporary interior, all-vinyl except for pattern cloth on portions of seats; optional Custom-Colored interiors.

All-steel body with four doors, load compartment, endgates. Crank-operated door windows and ventipanes; wraparound rear-quarter windows. High-quality safety glass. 6.70-15—6-ply rating tires.

Nine-passenger capacity. Foam-rubber-cushioned front seat. Three-place removable rear seat. Versatile center seat (one-place jump seat at right, two-passenger seat at left) folds fully to extend linoleum-surfaced platform. Vinyl-coated rubber floor mats.

Three-spoke steering wheel, horn ring, lighted lockable glove compartment, windshield wipers, sunshades, cigaret lighter, electric clock, built-in armrests on front doors, domelight with automatic door switches.

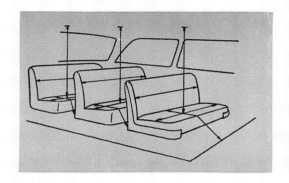

SITTING ROOM	Rear	Center	Front
Headroom	33.2"	34.9"	35.5"
Shoulder room	55.6"	56.5"	56.8"
Hiproom	46.4"	62.1"	62.0"
Legroom	39.0"	42.0"	43.5"
Seat adjustment			4.4"

VISION AREA . . . . 27.6 sq. ft.

LOAD CAPACITY . . . . 87.0 cu. ft.

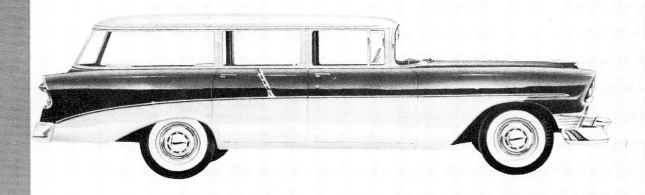

<table>
<tr><td>

CAR SIZE

Overall length	200.8" (16.7 ft.)
Overall width	74.0" (6.2 ft.)
Loaded height	60.8" (5.1 ft.)
Wheelbase	115.0" (9.6 ft.)
Wheel tread (av)	58.4" (4.9 ft.)
Ramp angles	Front 25°, Rear 15°
Road clearance, loaded	8.0"

</td></tr>
</table>

POWER AND WEIGHT

POWER TEAM	140-hp SIX	170-hp V8*	205-hp V8
Synchro-Mesh	3450 lb.	3420 lb.	3455 lb.
Overdrive	3480 lb.	3450 lb.	3485 lb.
Powerglide	3550 lb.	3520 lb.	3555 lb.

Add 130 lb. for gas and water, 150 for each passenger.

*162-hp with Synchro-Mesh or Overdrive

"TWO-TEN" BEAUVILLE (Nine-Passenger Station Wagon)

MODEL 2119

DISTINGUISHING FEATURES

A highly usable country car that really *goes to town*. Eight solid solors; 11 two-tones with conventional or Speedline color styling. All-vinyl charcoal-and-ivory Contemporary interior; optional Custom-Colored interiors.

All-steel body with four doors, large load compartment, convenient endgates, and *three* three-passenger seats: driver's seat, versatile center seat, and removable rear seat. Either the jump seat section or the two-place section of the middle seat, or both, fold fully to extend the linoleum-surfaced cargo platform. Vinyl-coated rubber floor mats. Crank-operated door windows and ventipanes; wraparound rear-quarter windows. High-quality safety glass.

Two-spoke steering wheel with horn ring, lighted lockable glove compartment, two windshield wipers, two sunshades, cigaret lighter, front ashtray, applied front door-pull armrests, central domelight with automatic switches at both front doors.

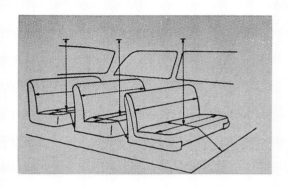

SITTING ROOM	Rear	Center	Front
Headroom	33.2"	34.9"	35.5"
Shoulder room	55.6"	56.5"	56.8"
Hiproom	46.4"	62.1"	62.0"
Legroom	39.0"	42.0"	43.5"
Seat adjustment			4.4"

VISION AREA	27.6 sq. ft.
LOAD CAPACITY	87.0 cu. ft.

CAR SIZE

Overall length	200.8" (16.7 ft.)
Overall width	74.0" (6.2 ft.)
Loaded height	60.8" (5.1 ft.)
Wheelbase	115.0" (9.6 ft.)
Wheel tread (av)	58.4" (4.9 ft.)
Ramp angles	Front 25°, Rear 15°
Road clearance, loaded	8.0"

POWER AND WEIGHT

POWER TEAM	140-hp SIX	170-hp V8*	205-hp V8
Synchro-Mesh	3405 lb.	3375 lb.	3410 lb.
Overdrive	3435 lb.	3405 lb.	3440 lb.
Powerglide	3505 lb.	3475 lb.	3510 lb.

Add 130 lb. for gas and water, 150 for each passenger.

*162-hp with Synchro-Mesh or Overdrive

"TWO-TEN" TOWNSMAN

DISTINGUISHING FEATURES

Ideal transportation for modern suburban living. Eight solid colors; 11 two-tones in conventional or Speedline color styling. All-vinyl charcoal-and-ivory Contemporary interior; optional Custom-Colored interiors.

All-steel body with large load compartment, convenient endgates, four doors for curb-side loading. Crank-operated door windows and ventipanes; wraparound rear-quarter windows. High-quality safety glass.

Two full-width seats for six (front seat foam-rubber-cushioned); rear seat folds level with linoleum-surfaced load platform. Seat cushions and backrests upholstered in an attractive vinyl with an irregular patch pattern. Vinyl-coated rubber floor mats.

Two-spoke steering wheel with horn ring, two windshield wipers, two sunshades, lighted lockable glove compartment, ashtray, front-seat armrests, cigaret lighter, coat hooks, and a central domelight with automatic switches at both front doors.

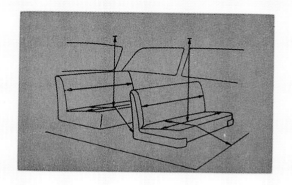

SITTING ROOM	Rear	Front
Headroom	35.2"	35.8"
Shoulder room	56.5"	56.8"
Hiproom	61.5"	62.0"
Legroom	44.6"	43.7"
Total seat adjustment		4.4"

VISION AREA	27.6 sq. ft.
LOAD CAPACITY	87.0 cu. ft.

CAR SIZE

Overall length	200.8" (16.7 ft.)
Overall width	74.0" (6.2 ft.)
Loaded height	59.4" (4.9 ft.)
Wheelbase	115.0" (9.6 ft.)
Wheel tread (av)	58.4" (4.9 ft.)
Ramp angles	Front 25°, Rear 15°
Road clearance, loaded	8.0"

POWER AND WEIGHT

POWER TEAM	140-hp SIX	170-hp V8*	205-hp V8
Synchro-Mesh	3425 lb.	3395 lb.	3430 lb.
Overdrive	3455 lb.	3425 lb.	3460 lb.
Powerglide	3525 lb.	3495 lb.	3530 lb.

Add 130 lb. for gas and water, 150 for each passenger.

*162-hp with Synchro-Mesh or Overdrive

DISTINGUISHING FEATURES

The station wagon with a sports car flair. 13 two-tones with Speedline color styling, or solid Onyx Black. Charcoal-and-ivory Contemporary interior; optional Custom-Colored interiors.

All-steel body with large doors and end-gates; grooved Turret Top. Crank-operated ventipanes and door windows; wraparound rear-quarter windows with sliding forward sections. High-quality safety glass.

Foam-rubber-cushioned seats for six: center-fold front seat; folding rear seat. Vinyl and pattern cloth interior. Perforated vinyl headlining; chrome roof bows. Deep-pile carpets. Linoleum-surfaced load platform.

Three-spoke wheel, horn ring, windshield wipers, sunshades, lighted lockable glove box, electric clock, cigaret lighter, ashtrays, front armrests, coat hooks. Two domelights with switches on instrument panel and at endgates—plus automatic door switches.

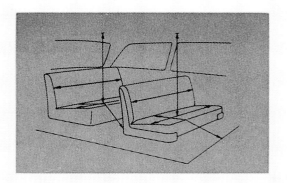

SITTING ROOM	Rear	Front
Headroom	34.6"	35.1"
Shoulder Room	56.0"	56.8"
Hiproom	61.5"	62.0"
Legroom	43.9"	43.4"
Total seat adjustment		4.4"

VISION AREA . . . . 25.2 sq. ft.

LOAD CAPACITY . . . . 71.0 cu. ft.

CAR SIZE

Overall length . . . . 200.8" (16.7 ft.)
Overall width . . . . 74.0" (6.2 ft.)
Loaded height . . . . 60.8" (5.1 ft.)
Wheelbase . . . . 115.0" (9.6 ft.)
Wheel tread (av) . . . . 58.4" (4.9 ft.)
Ramp angles . . . . Front 25°, Rear 15°
Road clearance, loaded . . . . 8.0"

POWER AND WEIGHT

POWER TEAM	140-hp SIX	170-hp V8*	205-hp V8
Synchro-Mesh	3355 lb.	3325 lb.	3360 lb.
Overdrive	3385 lb.	3355 lb.	3390 lb.
Powerglide	3455 lb.	3425 lb.	3460 lb.

Add 130 lb. for gas and water, 150 for each passenger.
*162-hp with Synchro-Mesh or Overdrive

"TWO-TEN" HANDYMAN

DISTINGUISHING FEATURES

A six-passenger family car that doubles as a hard-working pickup. Eight solid color selections; 11 two-tones in conventional or Speedline color styling. All-vinyl charcoal-and-ivory Contemporary interior; optional Customer-Colored interiors.

All-steel body with big load compartment, endgates, extra-large doors. Crank-operated door windows, center windows, and ventipanes. Wraparound rear-quarter windows. High-quality safety glass.

Foam rubber-cushioned front seat with center-fold backrests; folding rear seat forms forward extension of linoleum-surfaced load platform. Seat cushions and backrests in attractive vinyl with irregular patch pattern. Vinyl-coated rubber floor mats.

Two-spoke steering wheel, horn ring, windshield wipers, sunshades, lighted lockable glove compartment, cigaret lighter, ashtray, door-pull front-seat armrests, and a central domelight with automatic door switches.

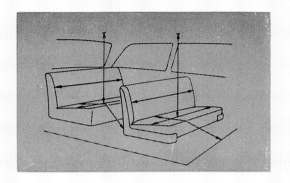

SITTING ROOM	Rear	Front
Headroom	35.2"	35.5"
Shoulder room	56.5"	56.8"
Hiproom	61.5"	62.0"
Legroom	44.6"	43.7"
Total seat adjustment		4.4"

VISION AREA . . . . 28.1 sq. ft.

LOAD CAPACITY . . . . 87.0 cu. ft.

CAR SIZE

Overall length................................200.8" (16.7 ft.)
Overall width.................................74.0" (6.2 ft.)
Loaded height................................60.8" (5.1 ft.)
Wheelbase....................................115.0" (9.6 ft.)
Wheel tread (av)............................58.4" (4.9 ft.)
Ramp angles.......................Front 25°, Rear 15°
Road clearance, loaded......................8.0"

POWER AND WEIGHT

POWER TEAM	140-hp SIX	170-hp V8*	205-hp V8
Synchro-Mesh	3335 lb.	3305 lb.	3340 lb.
Overdrive	3365 lb.	3335 lb.	3370 lb.
Powerglide	3435 lb.	3405 lb.	3440 lb.

Add 130 lb. for gas and water, 150 for each passenger.

*162-hp with Synchro-Mesh or Overdrive

MODELS

DISTINGUISHING FEATURES

The thriftiest of station wagons—with the extra-low silhouette of all Chevrolet station wagons. Six solid colors; six two-tones with either conventional or Speedline color styling. Tough, washable all-vinyl interior in gold with charcoal or gold with green.

All-steel body with big load compartment. large doors, endgates. Crank-operated door windows, ventipanes; wraparound rear-quarter windows. High-quality safety glass.

Two full-width seats, seating six; center-fold front-seat backrests; folding rear seat forms forward extension of load platform. Cushions and backrests of textured vinyl. Bolsters, gold ribbed-vinyl; facings, gold plain-surfaced vinyl. Sidewalls duplicate seat materials. Black rubber floor mats; black or green platform linoleum.

Two-spoke steering wheel, horn button, windshield wipers, sunshade, instrument panel ashtray, lockable glove compartment, central domelight operated by main light switch.

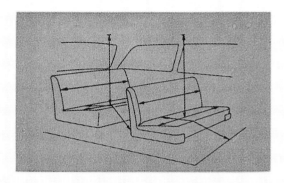

SITTING ROOM	Rear	Front
Headroom	35.2"	35.5"
Shoulder room	56.5"	56.8"
Hiproom	61.5"	62.0"
Legroom	44.6"	43.7"
Total seat adjustment		4.4"

VISION AREA . . . . 27.8 sq. ft.

LOAD CAPACITY . . . . 87.0 cu. ft

Accelerator-pedal cover, Rubber . . . . Accessory
Air cleaner, Oil bath . . . . Option 216
Air conditioner (V8 models) . . . . . . Acc. or Opt. 450
Armrests ("One-Fifty" models) . . . . Accessory
Autronic Eye . . . . Accessory (On special order)

Backup lights . . . . Accessory
Body sill moldings, Chrome . . . . Accessory
Brake signal light, Parking . . . . Accessory
Brakes, Power . . . . Accessory or Option 412

Cigaret lighter with socket light . . . . Accessory
Clock, Electric ("Two-Ten" and
    "One-Fifty" models) . . . . Accessory
Clutch, Heavy-duty (11-inch dia.) . . . . . Option 227
Colors, Optional convertible-top . . . . See color chart
Colors, Optional exterior . . . . See color chart
Compass, Illuminated . . . . Accessory
Courtesy lights, Inside . . . . Accessory
Custom-Colored interiors . . . . See color chart

Door edge guards, Chrome . . . . Accessory
Door handle shields, Chrome . . . . Accessory

Engine, "Super Turbo-Fire V8" . . . . Option 410
Engine, V8 (with Overdrive) . . . . Option 222
Engine, V8 (with Powerglide) . . . . Option 223
Engine, V8 (with Synchro-Mesh) . . . . . . Option 221
Exhaust extension, Chrome . . . . Accessory

Fender guards, Chrome . . . . Accessory
Fender-top moldings, Chrome front . . . . Accessory
Fender shields, Chrome front . . . . Accessory
Floor mats, Contoured rubber
    (Six colors) . . . . Accessory
Floor mats, Flat rubber (Four colors) . . . Accessory

Gasoline tank filler cap, Locking . . . . . . Accessory
Generator, 30-ampere . . . . Option 325
Generator, 40-ampere low cut-in . . . . . . Option 325
Glass, E-Z-Eye tinted safety . . . . Option 398
Glove compartment automatic light
    ("One-Fifty" models) . . . . Accessory
Governor, Six-cylinder engine . . . . Option 241

Heater and defroster, De Luxe . . . . Dealer- or
                                factory-installed accessory
Heater and defroster, Recirculating . . . . Dealer- or
                                factory-installed accessory
Horn, Vibrator . . . . Accessory
License frame, Chrome . . . . Accessory
Lift, Convertible-top . . . . Accessory
Mirror, Vanity sunshade . . . . Accessory
Oil filter (Six-cylinder models) . . . . Option 237
Oil filter, Full-flow
    (V8 models) . . . . . . Factory optional accessory 104
Radiator grille and front-fender guard,
    Chrome . . . . Accessory

Radiator insect screen.................Accessory
Radio antenna, Front-fender...........with radio
Radio antenna adapter, Rear-fender.....Accessory
Radio, Manual-tuning...   ....Accessory
Radio, Pushbutton....................Accessory
Radio, Signal-seeking...............Accessory
Radio speaker, Rear..................Accessory
Rain deflectors, Chrome side window....Accessory
Rearview mirror, Inside nonglare........Accessory
Rearview mirror, Outside body-mount...Accessory
Rearview mirror, Outside remote-control.Accessory

Seat, Power-controlled (Bel Air and
   "Two-Ten" models)...............Option 397
Seat covers, Fiber.....................Accessory
Seat covers, Nylon....................Accessory
Seat covers, Plastic....................Accessory
Seat cushion covers, Nylon ....Accessory
Seat pad, Ventilated...................Accessory
Shaver, Electric......................Accessory
Spotlight, Portable....................Accessory
Spotlight, Remote-control
   (with rearview mirror)..............Accessory
Springs, Chassis heavy-duty rear.......Option 254
Steering, Power.....................Option 324
Sunshade, Right-side ("One-Fifty").....Accessory

Tires, Blackwall (6.70-15, 6-ply).......Option 288

Tires, Blackwall (7.10-15, 4-ply)......Option 297
Tires, Whitewall (6.70-15, 4 ply)......Option 290
Tires, Whitewall (6.70-15, 6-ply)......Option 288
Tires, Whitewall (7.10-15, 4-ply)......Option 297
Tissue dispenser, Chrome............Accessory
Tool kit............................Accessory
Traffic light viewer...................Accessory
Transmission, Overdrive.............Option 315
Transmission, Powerglide............Option 313
Trunk light.........................Accessory

Underhood light.....................Accessory

Wheel carrier, Continental............Accessory
Wheel covers, Chrome wire
   ("Two-Ten" and "One-Fifty" models).Accessory
Wheel covers, De Luxe chrome.........Accessory
Wheel disks, Chrome ("Two-Ten" and
   "One-Fifty" models)................Accessory
Windows, Power-controlled (Bel Air
   and "Two-Ten" models)...........Option 426
Windshield glare shield, Plastic.........Accessory
Windshield outside sun visor...........Accessory
Windshield washer...................Accessory
Windshield washer, Foot-operated......Accessory
Windshield wiper blade, De-icing.......Accessory
Windshield wipers, Dual electric.......Option 320
Wiring junction block................Accessory

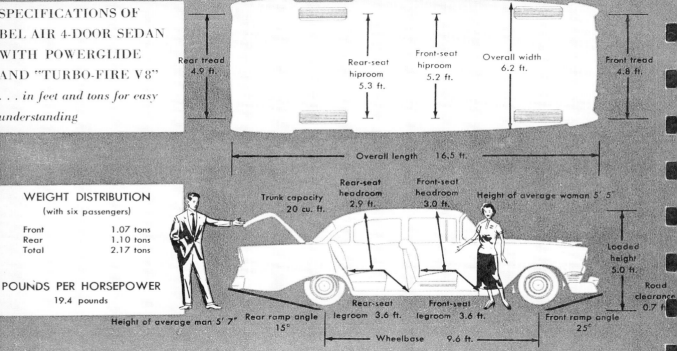

SPECIFICATIONS OF
BEL AIR 4-DOOR SEDAN
WITH POWERGLIDE
AND "TURBO-FIRE V8"
. . . in feet and tons for easy
understanding

Rear tread 4.9 ft.

Rear-seat hiproom 5.3 ft.

Front-seat hiproom 5.2 ft.

Overall width 6.2 ft.

Front tread 4.8 ft.

Overall length 16.5 ft.

WEIGHT DISTRIBUTION

(with six passengers)

Front	1.07 tons
Rear	1.10 tons
Total	2.17 tons

POUNDS PER HORSEPOWER

19.4 pounds

Trunk capacity 20 cu. ft.

Rear-seat headroom 2.9 ft.

Front-seat headroom 3.0 ft.

Height of average woman 5' 5"

Loaded height 5.0 ft.

Road clearance 0.7 ft.

Height of average man 5' 7"

Rear ramp angle 15°

Rear-seat legroom 3.6 ft.

Front-seat legroom 3.6 ft.

Front ramp angle 25°

Wheelbase 9.6 ft.

SIZE

Sized for Comfort and Maneuverability

- Plenty of passenger room—for comfort
- Lots of luggage space—for convenience
- Big windows all around—for safer vision
- Big doorways with low steps—for ease of entry and graceful exit
- Compact overall length and width and small turning circle—for easy handling
- Low overall height—for good appearance
- Steep ramp angles—for going up and down driveways and other grades
- Ample road clearance and nearly equal treads—for travelling any road
- Broad wheel treads, wide spring centers, and low center of gravity—for stability
- Balanced weight distribution—with seats cradled between the wheels—for riding ease
- Exceptionally light car weight per horsepower—for lively, thrifty performance
- Extra-large brakes—for quick stopping

INSIDE ROOMINESS FOR COMFORT, COMPACT EXTERIOR FOR HANDLING EASE, *AND LOADED WITH POWER FOR SAFER PERFORMANCE!*

COMPARABLE MODEL DIMENSIONS

Specifications common to all models

- **Horsepower:** 140-hp Six, 162-hp V8, 170-hp V8 (with Powerglide), 205-hp V8
- **Brake Dia.:** 11″
- **Wheelbase:** 115″
- **Tread:** Front 58″, Rear 58.8″
- **Turning Dia.:** 41.5 ft.
- **Ramp Angles:** Front 25°, Rear 15°
- **Road Clearance** (**): 8″

Model	Passengers	Load Space (cu. ft.)	Dry Weight* (lb.)	Length	Width	Height**	FS Headroom	FS Legroom	FS Hiproom	FS Shoulder	RS Headroom***	RS Legroom***	RS Hiproom***	RS Shoulder***	Front Doorway Height	FD Width Above Belt	FD Width Below Belt	FD Step Height	Rear Doorway Height	RD Width	RD Step Height	Vision Area (sq. ft.)
4-DOOR SEDANS																						
BEL AIR SEDAN	6	20	3235	197.5″	74″	60.5″	35.6″	43.7″	62.0″	56.8″	35.1″	42.6″	63.0″	56.6″	42.0″	28.0″	37.0″	14.0″	41.0″	27.5″	14.3″	24.4
"TWO-TEN" SEDAN	6	20	3220	197.5″	74″	60.5″	35.6″	43.7″	62.0″	56.8″	35.1″	42.6″	63.0″	56.6″	42.0″	28.0″	37.0″	14.0″	41.0″	27.5″	14.3″	24.4
"ONE-FIFTY" SEDAN	6	20	3195	197.5″	74″	60.5″	35.6″	43.7″	62.0″	56.8″	35.1″	42.6″	63.0″	56.6″	42.0″	28.0″	37.0″	14.0″	41.0″	27.5″	14.3″	24.4
2-DOOR SEDANS																						
BEL AIR SEDAN	6	20	3195	197.5″	74″	60.5″	35.6″	43.7″	62.0″	56.8″	35.1″	42.6″	63.0″	56.6″	42.0″	34.0″	43.8″	14.0″	None	None	None	24.7
"TWO-TEN" SEDAN	6	20	3185	197.5″	74″	60.5″	35.6″	43.7″	62.0″	56.8″	35.1″	42.6″	63.0″	56.6″	42.0″	34.0″	43.8″	14.0″	None	None	None	24.7
"TWO-TEN" CLUB COUPE	6	20	3185	197.5″	74″	60.5″	35.6″	43.7″	62.0″	56.8″	35.1″	42.6″	63.0″	56.6″	42.0″	34.0″	43.8″	14.0″	None	None	None	24.7
"ONE-FIFTY" SEDAN	6	20	3155	197.5″	74″	60.5″	35.6″	43.7″	62.0″	56.8″	35.1″	42.6″	63.0″	56.6″	42.0″	34.0″	43.8″	14.0″	None	None	None	24.7
"ONE-FIFTY" UTILITY SEDAN	3	51	3120	197.5″	74″	60.5″	35.6″	43.7″	62.0″	56.8″	None	None	None	None	42.0″	34.0″	43.8″	14.0″	None	None	None	24.6
SPORT MODELS																						
BEL AIR SPORT SEDAN	6	20	3290	197.5″	74″	59.1″	33.6″	43.5″	61.7″	56.0″	33.6″	41.8″	62.9″	56.8″	42.0″	27.8″	37.5″	14.0″	41.0″	38.0″	14.3″	22.9
"TWO-TEN" SPORT SEDAN	6	20	3285	197.5″	74″	59.1″	33.6″	43.5″	61.7″	56.0″	33.6″	41.8″	62.9″	56.8″	42.0″	27.8″	37.5″	14.0″	41.0″	38.0″	14.3″	22.9
BEL AIR SPORT COUPE	6	20	3225	197.5″	74″	59.1″	34.4″	43.4″	61.7″	56.8″	33.9″	38.5″	54.2″	56.7″	40.0″	32.0″	43.0″	14.0″	None	None	None	23.1
"TWO-TEN" SPORT COUPE	6	20	3225	197.5″	74″	59.1″	34.4″	43.4″	61.7″	56.8″	33.9″	38.5″	50.1″	56.7″	40.0″	32.0″	43.0″	14.0″	None	None	None	23.1
BEL AIR CONVERTIBLE	5	17	3350	197.5″	74″	59.1″	34.2″	43.4″	61.7″	56.8″	34.0″	38.7″	48.4″	56.7″	40.0″	32.0″	43.0″	14.0″	None	None	None	19.7
STATION WAGONS – 4-DOOR																						
BEL AIR BEAUVILLE	9	87	3475	200.8″	74″	60.8″	35.5″	43.5″	62.0″	56.8″	34.9″, 33.2″	42.0″, 39.0″	62.1″, 46.4″	55.5″, 55.6″	42.0″	28.0″	37.0″	15.0″	41.0″	27.5″	15.3″	27.6
"TWO-TEN" BEAUVILLE	6	87	3450	200.8″	74″	60.8″	35.5″	43.5″	62.0″	56.8″	34.9″, 33.2″	42.0″, 39.0″	62.1″, 46.4″	55.5″, 55.6″	42.0″	28.0″	37.0″	15.0″	41.0″	27.5″	15.3″	27.6
"TWO-TEN" TOWNSMAN	6	87	3405	200.8″	74″	60.8″	35.8″	43.7″	62.0″	56.8″	35.2″	44.6″	61.5″	56.5″	42.0″	28.0″	37.0″	15.0″	41.0″	27.5″	15.3″	27.6
BEL AIR NOMAD	6	71	3425	200.8″	74″	59.4″	35.1″	43.4″	62.0″	56.8″	34.6″	43.9″	61.5″	56.0″	41.5″	34.0″	43.8″	15.0″	None	None	None	25.2
STATION WAGONS – 2-DOOR																						
"TWO-TEN" HANDYMAN	6	87	3355	200.8″	74″	60.8″	35.5″	43.7″	62.0″	56.8″	35.2″	44.6″	61.5″	56.5″	42.0″	34.0″	43.8″	15.0″	None	None	None	28.1
"ONE-FIFTY" HANDYMAN	6	87	3335	200.8″	74″	60.8″	35.5″	43.7″	62.0″	56.8″	35.2″	44.6″	61.5″	56.5″	42.0″	34.0″	43.8″	15.0″	None	None	None	27.8

* … with … automatic transmission **Car fully loaded ***Center and rear seats for Beauvilles

The 1956 Chevrolet is revolutionary. Not only does it outclass all cars in its field, but it steals the thunder from higher priced cars in features, styling, utility, and ability.

Nearly every person considers his automobile to be one of his proudest possessions. He may admire it for any or all of its many fine features but, when he considers why he bought it, two bedrock fundamentals stand out. These are the car's *utility* and *ability*: utility in the sense of the room it provides for him and his passengers, ability in the sense of its performance. Some cars are big—with a sacrifice in ability; others are small—with a sacrifice in utility. In the 1956 Chevrolet, however, sound engineering has resulted in a car that has ideal proportions—in size, weight, and power—to provide an ideal combination of utility and ability. Not only is this car big inside for comfort, but it's compact outside for enviable maneuverability and it's loaded with power for record-breaking performance.

This ideal combination stems from the car's compact design. Compactness in the sides broadens the interior yet decreases the car width. Compactness in the chassis and body makes the car low for better roadability and appearance, with a low hood and deck that make the road immediately ahead and behind the car easy to see. Compactness ahead of the front wheels and behind the rear wheels keeps the overhang small; avoids excessive length that makes maneuvering hard. For stability, not only is the center of gravity low, but the wheel treads and spring centers are broad in relation to the car width. Likewise, the wheelbase is long for the car length. Compact design also pares dead weight to the bone, and with Chevrolet's great power, provides a very low weight-to-power ratio.

Compact
Design

SIZE

INTERIOR ROOMINESS

In its field, the Chevrolet provides enviable sitting room, not only in width of seats but also in headroom and legroom. For easy entrance, its doorways are large, with low doorsteps, and its large windows contribute to comfort and safety. In relation to higher priced cars, the Chevrolet compares most favorably in roominess.

Window Areas (sq. ft.)	Windshield	Side Windows	Rear Window	All Around
4-Door Sedan	7.1	9.9	7.4	24.4
2-Door Sedan	7.1	10.2	7.4	24.7
Utility Sedan	7.1	10.1	7.4	24.6
Sport Sedan	6.8	8.6	7.3	22.7
Sport Coupe	6.8	9.0	7.3	23.1
Convertible	6.8	8.1	4.8	19.7
Beauville	7.1	16.7	3.8	27.6
Townsman	7.1	16.7	3.8	27.6
Nomad	6.8	9.7	4.5	25.2
Handyman	7.1	17.1	3.8	28.0

Windows

SPACIOUS TRUNKS

Although trunk proportions differ in conventional and sport models, fully 20 cubic feet of space is provided in each—except the convertible in which three cubic feet are taken up by the top well.

Luggage and Cargo Space

All dimensions given below are in inches.

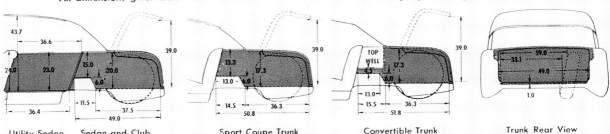

Utility Sedan Load Space   Sedan and Club Coupe Trunk

Sport Coupe Trunk

Convertible Trunk

Trunk Rear View (All Models)

SIZE

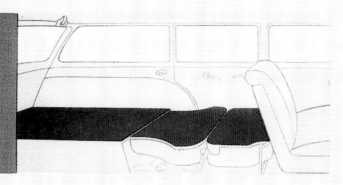

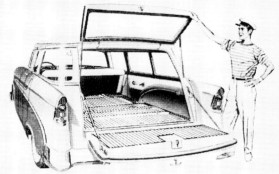

AMPLE DIMENSIONS

	All Conventiona STATION WAGONS* Folding Seat Up	Folding Seat Down	BEL AIR NOMAD Folding Seat Up	Folding Seat Down
Platform length to tailgate	47.0"	84.4"	43.0"	74.3"
Platform length to tailgate end	68.7"	106.1"	65.6"	96.9"
Maximum load space width	58.3"	58.3"	56.4"	56.4"
Width between wheelhouses	46.1"	46.1"	46.3"	46.3"
Height—platform to top	36.9"	36.9"	35.0"	35.0"
Capacity—to window sills (cu ft)	45.0"	87.0"	36.0"	71.0"

LARGE REAR OPENING

	All Conventional STATION WAGONS	BEL AIR NOMAD
Width	43.5"	41.8"
Height	28.3"	28.4"
Approximate tailgate loading height with vehicle empty	30.0"	30.0"

* Dimensions for 9-passenger station wagons, with rear seat removed, are same as for other conventional station wagons.

SIZE

COMPACT EXTERIOR

Car
Length
and
Width

Great length and width in a car can be serious handicaps under many conditions of modern-day driving. The 197.5″ Chevrolet overall length (200.8″ in station wagons) is compact in relation to the wheel base (115″). Also the Chevrolet overall width (74″) is compact in relation to the broad interior. As the result, maneuvering in today's multi-lane traffic is easier with the Chevrolet than with cars having larger exteriors and the Chevrolet can be parked in spaces that are too short for cars that are less compactly designed.

Ramp
Angles

Overhang is the length between the bumper and wheel center at each end of the car. Because Chevrolet's overhang, both front and rear, is short, the car's ramp angles are large—so it can go up driveway ramps and other short inclines and can come down slopes that longer cars might scrape.

Car Stability

With modern scientific engineering, the weight of a car has little to do with its stability. A low center of gravity and a broad rear suspension provide the road-keeping qualities formerly obtained by heavy, cumbersome construction.

Center of Gravity

The center of gravity is the point above the road at which an automobile balances—and the lower the center of gravity, the greater the car stability. In the 1956 Chevrolet, many factors make the center of gravity extra low. The double-drop frame, close integration of the frame and the body, Hotchkiss drive, hypoid axle, and Outrigger rear suspension permit a low body location. With body, seats, and passengers low, the greater weight of the car is low.

Treads and Suspension

To give the Chevrolet a wide-based support, its treads (width between wheel centers at road level) are extra broad and the rear springs are mounted outside the frame next to the wheels. In addition to being extra broad, the treads are practically equal (58″ front, 58.8″ rear), making tracking easier under all road conditions. Another valuable factor is Chevrolet's high (8″) road clearance, the height from a level road to the axle center with the car loaded.

Road Clearance

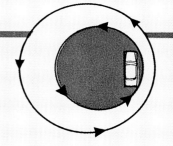

The Chevrolet's compact length and width, with superior steering geometry, result in small turning circles: 41.5 feet diameter (curb to curb), 44.5 feet diameter (wall to wall). Hence the Chevrolet can turn in places that are too narrow for bigger cars to turn in.

Turning Circle

SIZE

BALANCED WEIGHT

No one ordinarily would consider buying a car by the pound, like beefsteak, but it's a wise precaution because the *cost per pound* is a good indicator of the car's relative value—one which automotive executives use consistently. On this basis alone, a Chevrolet is the best value. Although the quality of the Chevrolet is high, it costs up to approximately 68 percent *less per pound* than other makes. This is because Chevrolet produces so many more vehicles that it can pass on to the customer substantial savings from mass manufacturing and purchasing—without sacrifice in quality.

Car weight, under varying conditions, is called by various names. The weight of the car alone, without passengers, load, gasoline and water is called *shipping weight* or *dry weight*. The weight of the empty car ready to drive, with the cooling system and gas tank filled is called *curb weight*. The weight of the fully loaded car, with passengers, gasoline and water, is called *loaded weight*.

In addition to a low cost per pound, Chevrolet saves money for the customer—in initial cost and in operating costs throughout the life of the car—by the elimination of weight *where it is unnecessary*. For example, if the engines were removed from cars in the low-price field and the cars then were weighed, it would be found that the Chevrolet is the heavier car—because it is structurally more substantial. Chevrolet believes the extra weight in the car structure *is necessary* because it contributes to safety. On the other hand, if the cars were weighed with V8 engines installed it would be found that the other cars weigh more. This is because their V8 engines weigh more than Chevrolet's compact V8. Chevrolet believes extra weight of this nature *is unnecessary* because it contributes nothing to the car's performance and adds weight on the car's front-end to disturb the car balance.

Cost per pound

Definitions of Weight

Necessary and Unnecessary Car Weight

Both Chevrolet engine types weigh about the same (V8, 506 lb.; Six, 550 lb.) so there is no appreciable difference in weight that might upset the car's balance whether a six or V8 engine is installed. The engine weights in combination with the weights of the various transmissions that are available result in the following powerplant weights:

<table>
<tr><th></th><th>Conventional</th><th>Overdrive</th><th>Automatic</th></tr>
<tr><td>V8</td><td>570 lb.</td><td>597 lb.</td><td>665 lb.</td></tr>
<tr><td>Six</td><td>611 lb.</td><td>639 lb.</td><td>708 lb.</td></tr>
</table>

Engine and Powerplant Weights

Weight distribution is the proportions of the total car weight borne by the front and rear wheels, and is determined by weighing the front and rear ends of the car separately. When these weights are approximately the same, the weight distribution is considered to be balanced. Balanced weight distribution provides a better ride, safer, easier handling, and easier maneuverability. Weight distribution varies with the use of different power teams. For instance, the weight distribution (lb.) of the Bel Air 4-door sedan, loaded with six passengers, gasoline and water, varies as follows:

Weight Distribution

<table>
<tr><th colspan="2">Standard Six</th><th colspan="2">Standard V8</th><th colspan="2">Powerglide Six</th><th colspan="2">Powerglide V8</th></tr>
<tr><th>Front</th><th>Rear</th><th>Front</th><th>Rear</th><th>Front</th><th>Rear</th><th>Front</th><th>Rear</th></tr>
<tr><td>2090</td><td>2170</td><td>2065</td><td>2170</td><td>2170</td><td>2190</td><td>2140</td><td>2190</td></tr>
</table>

These weight distributions are all nearly ideal. Competitive cars which claim balanced weight distribution do not always have it with all power teams. For instance, when they use a V8 engine with an automatic transmission in place of a six with conventional transmission, the weight on the front wheels is increased approximately 200 to 250 pounds, in contrast to 50 for the Chevrolet. Because their front wheels must carry an extra burden—about that of an extra passenger—steering and handling are harder and wear on the front tires is greater. To carry this extra weight, they recommend higher tire pressures than with their sixes. Chevrolet's tire pressure is uniform for every tire, whether the engine is a six or a V8, for softer, smoother riding and more stable handling and steering.

Tire Pressure

GREATER POWER

In 1955, Chevrolet amazed the nation with its spectacular performance. In NASCAR* trial after NASCAR trial, stock Chevrolets out-performed all low- and medium-priced cars and every high-priced car but one. This was due in part to Chevrolet's very low weight-to-power ratio. The truest indicator of a car's relative ability is its weight-to-power ratio. Dividing the car weight in pounds by the maximum horsepower of its engine shows the number of pounds each horsepower must pull; and the lower the ratio, the better the car's performance. For 1956, the Chevrolet weighs but little more (about 35 pounds), but improvements in its engines boost the horsepower substantially. The result: even lower ratios, even better performance.

National Association for Stock Car Auto Racing.

Weight-to-
Power
Ratio

HORSEPOWER INCREASES

	"Blue-Flame" 6	"Turbo-Fire V8"	"Super Turbo-Fire V8"
With Synchro-Mesh			
1956	140 hp	162 hp	205 hp
1955	123 hp	162 hp	180 hp
	+17 hp		+25 hp
With Overdrive			
1956	140 hp	162 hp	205 hp
1955	123 hp	162 hp	180 hp
	+17 hp		+25 hp
With Powerglide			
1956	140 hp	170 hp	205 hp
1955	136 hp	162 hp	180 hp
	+4 hp	+8 hp	+25 hp

SIZE

HOW BIG IS BIG?

Size, weight, and power are relative and can be appreciated only by actual comparison. Because Chevrolet's size, weight, and power are ideal, they serve as the *yardstick* by which all other cars are measured. By comparing Chevrolet model for model, weight for weight, power for power, and dimension for dimension with *any* other car, no matter what its price class, it is found that the Chevrolet has important advantages. Even when compared with the most expensive makes of cars, Chevrolet excels in many respects, as shown in the following chart. In this chart, one of the more expensive 1956 model *big cars* is compared with a comparably equipped Chevrolet Bel Air model.

COMPARABLE 4-DOOR SEDANS	BIG CAR	BEL AIR	BIG CAR ADVANTAGES	CHEVROLET ADVANTAGES
COST (%) with same equipment*	100	60		About half that of *big car*
DRY WEIGHT (lb.) as equipped* MAXIMUM HORSEPOWER POUNDS PER HORSEPOWER	4210 285 14.8	3370 205 16.4	Slightly better performance than Chevrolet	
BRAKE DIAMETER (in.) POUNDS PER INCH DIAMETER	12 357	11 306		Better braking with less pounds per inch of brake diameter
OVERALL LENGTH (ft.) OVERALL WIDTH (ft.) OVERALL HEIGHT, LOADED (ft.)	18.5 6.7 5.0	16.5 6.2 5.0		Easier to handle; fits in parking spaces too small for *big car*
WHEELBASE (ft.) and % length FRONT TREAD (ft.) and % width REAR TREAD (ft.) and % width	10.5 (56%) 4.9 (73%) 5.0 (75%)	9.6 (58%) 4.8 (77%) 4.9 (80%)		Greater stability and roadability than big car
TURNING DIAMETER (ft.) FRONT RAMP ANGLE (degrees) REAR RAMP ANGLE (degrees) ROAD CLEARANCE (in.)	48.5** 20 11 7	41.5 25 15 8		Turns in places too narrow for *big car*; goes up and down inclines *big car* scrapes
SITTING ROOM (in.) Headroom Legroom Hiproom	Front Rear 35.4 34.3 44.8 43.9 61.8 63.8	Front Rear 35.6 35.4 43.7 42.6 62.0 63.0	About one inch more legroom than Chevrolet	About same headroom and hiproom as *big car*

*V8 engine with dual exhausts, automatic transmission, and power steering.   **Estimated

SIZE

A TYPICAL CHEVROLET BEAUTY . . . THE 1956 BEL AIR 4-DOOR SPORT SEDAN!

Front-View Beauty
- Panoramic windshield
- Long, broad, low hood
- Eagle-motif hood ornament
- Smart hood emblem
- Hooded, recessed headlights
- Car-wide lattice grille
- Large parking lights
- Massive contoured bumper
- Bullet-type bumper guards

Profile Smartness
- Graceful Turret Top
- Large side windows
- Dipdown belt line
- Straight-through sides
- Long, level fender lines
- Series name in chrome
- Rakish wheel openings
- Full-width wheel disks
- Speedline chrome treatment

Rearview Fleetness
- Wide-Vista rear window
- Broad, low rear deck
- Smart rear deck emblem
- Prominent fender crowns
- Reverse-slope taillights
- Taillight gas tank filler
- Built-in accessory backup lights
- Massive contoured bumper
- Dual-purpose bumper guards

GLAMOROUS COLORS . . . IN LONG-LASTING POLISHED LACQUER . . . ACCENTED BY GLEAMING CHROME

EXTERIORS

TOMORROW'S STYLING TODAY . . .
FOR LONG-LASTING PRIDE OF OWNERSHIP!

The prominent styling features of a typical 1956 Chevrolet are shown
on the opposite page, as an example of Chevrolet's modern styling.

A BRAND-NEW APPEARANCE

Quick as a wink one can see that the 1956 Chevrolet is STYLISHLY NEW, excitingly distinctive! Just how new in looks the Chevrolet is, doesn't depend on where the eye focuses—it's new everywhere! Its captivating new lines . . . its just-right new decoration . . . its gay new colors and smart new color styling, soar the 1956 Chevrolet to new beauty heights that far exceed its price class. Yet, behind all this new car's new beauty there's purpose, for Chevrolet beauty is *functional* . . . with a purpose in every detail.

NEW FRONT-VIEW BEAUTY

Front-End
Styling

From the front, there's a new sense of road-hugging stability about the 1956 Chevrolet . . . a broader, lower, stronger look that imparts *big car* dignity as well as a challenging eagerness to take off and go. This is due in part to the completely new chrome parts that grace the front of the car.

Bumper
and
Radiator
Grille
Styling

Based on a huge contoured bumper, with bullet-shaped guards, Chevrolet's front-view beauty rises to a forward-jutting, car-wide lattice grille that curves with the bumper completely around to the wheel openings. The lattice is broad, with large apertures that permit entrance of an abundance of air to cool the engine. A bold, tapered molding frames the grille and encloses the rectangular parking lights (now almost as large as the headlights) which are safety-spaced in the outer plots of the grille. Forward-slanting hooded frames embellish and protect the parking lights. A section of the grille molding

is mounted on the hood's lower edge to protect it while the hood is being opened or closed. To further emphasize the massive front appearance, an accessory radiator grille and fender guard, that spans the width of the car, may be mounted on the bumper.

Accessory
Front-End
Guards

Outstanding functional beauty is evident in the more prominent headlight hoods. New in shape and with deeper recesses in the fender crowns, they form graceful canopies that slant forward at about the same angle as the grille. Within their recesses, chrome linings frame the lights. Unlike bolted-on hoods, these have no unsightly rust-promoting breaks. Beyond the beauty they add to the car, they help direct the light rays and shield the lights from snow and drippings that might ice the glass.

Headlight
Hoods

Attractive new accessory chrome moldings, mounted above the headlights on the fender tops, add to the sparkle of the new car.

Fender-top
Moldings

THE MASSIVE NEW FRONT-END STYLING

Hood
Styling

Another feature that is appreciably noticeable, because of its outstanding attractiveness, is the longer hood. Extending four inches farther forward between the fenders, at a slightly steeper slope and with a flatter crown, it adds impressively to the car's sleek new appearance. Made from a single panel of steel to effect its modern smooth design, it also avoids a central seam that must be capped to prevent potential rusting. Instead, the hood center is attractively decorated by an integral raised rib that extends from the windshield to the grille.

Hood
Ornament
and
Emblems

Adding just the right spicing of hood adornment in keeping with the car's overall modern styling, is a sleek chrome hood ornament of eagle motif, mounted low on the hood in a modern snugging manner. And, directly below, is a chrome-framed Chevrolet emblem in colorful plastic. To identify V8 and six-cylinder models, two sizes of emblems are used. The emblem for the six-cylinder cars is broad, in keeping with the sense of massiveness in the car; that for the V8 is a smaller version of the same emblem, centered within a widely flared chrome V. Identically appearing emblems on the rear of the car assure identification of the new Chevrolet—whether coming or going.

Crowning Chevrolet's head-on appearance is its big panoramic windshield. Permitting the finest vision possible, it also achieves for Chevrolet an outstanding style effect with its full sweep-around design. On Bel Air and "Two-Ten" models, a gleaming wide chrome molding frames the windshield. And, on Bel Air models, the chrome treatment is carried right around to the door openings by chrome moldings on the windshield pillars. New on "One-Fifty" models is the chrome molding that caps the rubber in which the glass is retained. It is similar to that of the other series but is slightly narrower. Typical of the high quality so evident in Chevrolets is the chrome finish of the Bel Air rearview mirror frame, in full view through the windshield.

Windshield
Styling

NEW REARVIEW FLEETNESS

Rear Bumper Styling

From the rear, as well as from the front, the 1956 Chevrolet conveys an impression of even greater massiveness and fleetness. The ends of the larger bumper are protectively higher and noticeably more attractive as they curve gracefully around the contours of the extended fenders in full wraparound style. Seated on the bumper center bar, the bumper guards contain built-in lights for the license, which is positioned low on the trunk lid. A car-wide accessory guard, matching the one for the front of the car, can be mounted on top of the bumper. To permit lowering the tailgate, the bumper guards of station wagons are structurally different from those of other models and the bumper center is recessed to provide a protective mounting for the license. A massive-looking chrome frame, available as an accessory, can be adjusted to fit the license of any state.

Rear Bumper Guards

Chevrolet's big new taillights are eye-arresting. Cut in at a reverse slope in the fenders, they provide a fleet profile as well as a distinctive rear identification. The arch-shaped chrome molding that frames each unit encloses a background of embossed metal on which the ruby-red taillight and white backup light lenses are mounted. The conical taillight lens dominates the design with brilliant simplicity. Housing the tail, stop, parking, and turn-signal lights, it may be seen from the side as well as from the rear.

Another of Chevrolet's advanced features, is the new concealed location of the gasoline tank filler cap within the left taillight. Not only does this design avoid the beauty-marring effect of an external door in a fender or an exposed cap, but it also places the filler high for easier filling. Through means of extra-durable hinging, the taillight is swung downward, after turning a small decorative latch located above the taillight lens, for convenient access to the filler.

In keeping with Chevrolet's modern, long, broad lines, the rear deck of the sedans and coupes is kept low. Level with the fenders just behind the rear window, it slopes slightly downward between the fenders—adding length to the fender crowns. The trunk lid is broad and extends down nearly to bumper level so that, when it is open, there is ease of access to the luggage compartment. In the station wagons, the endgates similarly slope gracefully down between the fenders to near-bumper level.

The attractive motif of the hood emblem is repeated in the rear emblem of all models except the Nomad. On six-cylinder models with trunks, indented finger grips at the base of the emblem provide for trunk-lid lifting ease; the V8's have concealed finger grips in the lower portion of the broad V emblem. A chrome T-handle serves to open the endgates of the conventional station wagons, whereas the Nomad employs a solid chrome handle with a pushbutton release. Since it is in a class by itself, the Nomad is

identified from the rear by its name in chrome script and the seven chrome vertical bars that ornament its tailgate, plus special V emblems below the taillights on V8 models.

Blended in with the graceful top lines, the wide-vista rear window is a huge expanse of polished glass, that varies in shape by model to add to the distinctive appearance of each of the many body types. That of all conventional sedans and the club coupe is the wraparound type, affording *see-through* vision through the car. The window of the sport coupes is the same type but is carried even farther around into the side, while that of the new sport sedans has a styling all its own, with an upper edge that extends right down to the belt line in an exciting and revealing manner. Chrome decoration of the rear window is like that of the windshield, with a wide molding around the glass of the "Two-Ten" and Bel Air models and a cap molding on the glass-retaining rubber of the "One-Fifties." Because of its nature, the vinyl-plastic rear window of the convertible

has no molding. Instead, the rear view of this model is brightened, when the top is up, by a continuation of the side window sill molding which extends across its deck, and when the top is down, by the chrome inside molding around the windshield sides and top. In the station wagons, rear vision is provided by the wraparound rear-quarter windows and the curved window in the liftgate. In the "Two-Ten" and Bel Air station wagons, the chrome moldings that edge the top and belt lines of the car sides are continued around the rear of the car to frame the rear window. In the Nomad, additional sparkle is provided by chrome plating the entire liftgate frame and the pillars at its sides.

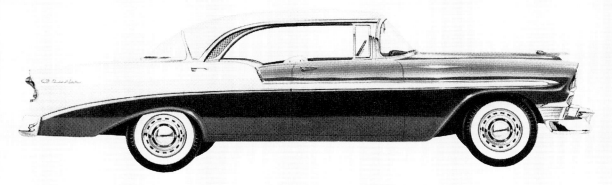

NEW PROFILE SMARTNESS

A look of fleeter mobility is gained by the Chevrolet's crisp, clean, new profile. The car looks longer, because it actually is longer —with an overall length of 16½ feet. And to go with this longer length, the car looks exceptionally low. And well it should, because the loaded height of the average Chevrolet for 1956 measures only five feet.

To emphasize these dimensions, the car's belt line is low. Above it, the body structure is light and airy; below it, straight-through side styling, with fenders that s-t-r-e-t-c-h from bumper to bumper, elongates the car lines. Adding further emphasis to the appearance of length is the effect of completely new, distinctive chrome and color styling.

EXTERIORS

AN AIRY UPPER STRUCTURE FOR EACH BODY TYPE

The gracefully contoured Turret Top of all models (except the convertible) is styled to appear shallow, belieing the tremendous strength its one-piece steel construction imparts to the entire car structure. A similar sense of shallowness is styled into the steel-tautened fabric of the convertible top. Heightening the sense of top shallowness is the *high-brow* effect achieved by carrying the curved contours of the well-sloped windshield and rear window high up into the top and far around into the body sides.

Enlarged by the shallowness of the top and the lowness of the belt line, exceptionally big side windows contribute, too, to the airiness of the upper structure. The super-strong pillars that join the top to the lower structure conversely are narrow, adding much to both visibility and airiness.

On each side, except for the handsome, chrome-framed, rectangular ventipane (standard in the front door of every model), the side window groups differ for each kind of body. In conventional four-door sedans, the large door windows are augmented by smart rear-quarter windows. In the conventional two-door sedans and club coupe, extra-large door and rear-quarter windows fill the same area as in the conventional four-door sedans. In the sport coupes, convertible, and the outstanding new sport sedans, the absence of center pillars between the top and belt line provides completely open sides. To reinforce the glass of these models and to prevent chipping of its edges, narrow chrome moldings edge each pane. Not only do these models (and the Nomad) look lower than the conventional models, but they are lower—by about $1\frac{1}{2}$ inches—to give them an even longer and much fleeter appearance.

In all conventional station wagons, wrap-around rear-quarter windows complete a wall of glass that extends around the car, uninterrupted except for the narrow body pillars. In the Nomad, however, a broad forward-slanting center pillar adds enchantment.

THREE GREAT SERIES . . .
and their marks of distinction!

The dazzling Bel Air

The distinctive "Two-Ten"

"The Beautiful "One-Fifty"

LONGER-LINE FENDERS

The fenders are extra long, making them all visible from the driver's seat to aid in guiding the car. With top lines that are more horizontal, they merge gracefully in the rear quarter of the body at a point which is enhanced, in sedans and coupes, by an attractive *dipdown* in the belt line. Below, rakish wheel openings sweep sharply rearward for a fleeting go-look even when standing still. Emphasizing Chevrolet's fleet appearance even more, is the distinctive front-fender *wind-crease* that sweeps from the headlight hood to blend into the flanged trailing edge of the front-wheel opening. Each rear fender is an integral part of the body from which it derives solidity. The possibility of a rusting seam also is avoided by integral construction, and a smoother appearance is gained. From the enhancing dipdown, past the rakish sweep of the higher wheel cutout, way back to the reverse slope of the taillight, the long rear-fender lines add to the new beauty of the Chevrolet.

NEW SIDE CHROME TREATMENTS

Window
Chrome
Moldings

The sills of all "Two-Ten" and Bel Air side windows are topped by chrome moldings. In addition, a rich effect is given to the sides of steel-topped Bel Air sedans and coupes by a molding that edges the top from the windshield to the base of the rear window. In Bel Air and "Two-Ten" station wagons, both the side and rear windows have chrome moldings that edge the top, as well as the window sills, around the car.

Side
Chrome
Moldings

Each series has its own chrome treatment on the car sides. "One-Fifty" models have a three-quarter length molding that extends back beyond the dipdown. At the dipdown it is joined by a diagonal sash molding—a feature now on *every* Chevrolet. "Two-Tens" have a full-length molding that arches gently down to the rear bumper. Bel Airs display this same molding but have a second molding above it which ends in the sash molding. Just ahead of each taillight, a chrome *Chevrolet*, or *Bel Air* with distinctive gold emblem, helps to identify each series.

Hub
Caps
and
Wheel
Disks

The rakish wheel openings disclose more of the wheels, making them more prominent. The chrome wheel disks of the Bel Airs display a spinner, surrounded by trademarks on a black background which, in turn, is encircled by black depressions simulating spokes. The hub caps are the same on "Two-Ten" and "One-Fifty" models—chrome with trademarks on a black background. To enhance the wheels of "Two-Ten" and "One-Fifty" models, Bel Air wheel disks may be substituted for the hub caps, or accessory chrome covers, that simulate wire wheels, may be used with the hub caps.

Side
Chrome
Accessories

Chrome accessories that are available for additional side embellishment include the front-fender stone guard, behind the wheel opening; the body sill molding, joining the wheel openings; door-handle shields, between the handles and doors; door-edge guards, on the rear edges of doors; and on conventional sedans, side window sun and rain deflectors.

NEW COLORS AND COLOR STYLING

Colors

The fashion is cheerful colors in striking arrangements. And, for 1956, Chevrolet provides one of the most magnificent selections of colors and arrangements ever offered—in 364 model-color combinations.

These combinations are based on fifteen colors which, except for the ever-popular black and ivory, are new colors that range through tones of gold, yellow, green, turquoise, blue, plum, red, beige, and gray (see color chart). Not only were they selected for their beauty, but months were spent in testing their resistance to sun and weather and salt spray to assure that their beauty would be long lasting. As well as being offered singly, they are tastefully combined in two optional styles: *conventional* styling and new *speedline* styling, made possible by *color breaks* provided by the new chrome.

Bel Air models are offered in single colors, or *speedline* two-tones that are doubly new because of the new colors and the new double chrome moldings on the car sides. In Bel Air sedans and coupes, the color that is used on the top, rear deck, and rear fenders also fills the space between the two moldings, while the remainder of the car is finished in the second color. In Bel Air station wagons, the second color also is used on the top. As a bonus with the Bel Air convertible, there is a choice of *two or more* top colors with every car color selection.

Bel Air Color Styling

"Two-Ten" and "One-Fifty" models are available in single colors, in *conventional* two-tones, in which one color is confined to the top with a second color below, and also in new, individual styles of *speedline* two-tones. In "Two-Tens," one color is used on the top and below the side moldings, with the second color in between. In "One-Fifty" models, one color is used on the top, rear deck, and below the side moldings; the other, on the hood, front fenders, and the body sides between the belt line and the moldings.

"Two-Ten" and "One-Fifty" Color Styling

A BEAUTIFUL FINISH . . . PROTECTED BY CHROME

All Chevrolet car colors are in highest quality, lustrous lacquer, applied in Chevrolet's famous *nine-step* finishing process that assures years of sparkling beauty. The nine steps include alkaline cleaning and rust-proofing, a primer coat, a glaze coat, wet sanding, three coats of pyroxylin lacquer, a sound-deadener application, and the machine polishing that gives the lasting luster. The lacquer is the same as on America's most expensive cars. When compared with synthetic enamel finishes, it is outstanding in every respect. It is smooth and uniform, without the *orange peel* surface of other finishes. It has greater richness and depth. (Even after neglect, its gloss can be restored to its original luster by polishing.) And if repairs must be made, they can be made better and more easily.

In addition to effective splash and gravel guards at the front and rear of the car; to help protect the car finish from hazards that beset all cars under modern driving conditions, Chevrolet uses more protective chrome than ever before. Chrome, or chromium, is a hard, durable metal, greatly resistant to corrosion. When plated on steel, or when alloyed with steel as in stainless steel moldings, it presents a surface that is not only gleamingly beautiful but also is much more durable than any paint. For this reason, Chevrolet uses chrome on all parts that are more subject to wear or damage: On bumpers, radiator grille, and hub caps—to protect them from bumping, scraping, and pitting by gravel; on handles, locks, and window sills—to protect them from scratching by rings or keys; in side moldings—to protect the finish from scraping by doors of other cars in parking lots; and in light rims—to protect the finish when lights are serviced or, as in the case of Chevrolet's new taillight gas tank filler—to protect the finish from chipping by gas pump nozzles.

Polished Lacquer Finish

Protective Chrome

1956 SOLID COLOR SELECTION

162 MODEL-COLOR COMBINATIONS IN 10 STRIKING SOLID COLORS

. . . with standard Contemporary Interior or optional Custom-Colored Interior as indicated in chart.

	Option No.	4-DOOR SEDANS			2-DOOR SEDANS					SPORT MODELS					STATION WAGONS 4-DOOR				2-DOOR	
		BEL AIR SEDAN	"TWO-TEN" SEDAN	"ONE-FIFTY" SEDAN	BEL AIR SEDAN	"TWO-TEN" SEDAN	"TWO-TEN" CLUB COUPE	"ONE-FIFTY" SEDAN	"ONE-FIFTY" UTILITY SEDAN	BEL AIR SPORT SEDAN	"TWO-TEN" SPORT SEDAN	BEL AIR SPORT COUPE	"TWO-TEN" SPORT COUPE	BEL AIR CONVERTIBLE	BEL AIR BEAUVILLE	"TWO-TEN" BEAUVILLE	"TWO-TEN" TOWNSMAN	BEL AIR NOMAD	"TWO-TEN" HANDYMAN	"ONE-FIFTY" HANDYMAN
Onyx BLACK	Std.	1A	1	2	1A	1	5	2	2	1A	1	1A	1	1Aa	1A	1	1	1A	1	3
Crocus YELLOW	523	1A	1	2	1A	1	5	2	2	1A	1	1A	1	1Aa	1A	1	1		1	3
Sherwood GREEN	506	1B	1C	2	1B	1C	5C	2	2	1B	1C	1B	1C	1Bc		1C	1C		1C	4
Pinecrest GREEN	504	1B	1C	2	1B	1C	5C	2	2	1B	1C	1B	1C	1Bb	1	1C	1C		1C	4
Harbor BLUE	510	1D	1E		1D	1E				1D	1E	1D	1E	1Dd						
Nassau BLUE	508	1D	1E	2	1D	1E	5	2	2	1D	1E	1D	1E	1Dd	1	1	1		1	3
Matador RED	522	1	1	2	1	1	5	2	2	1F	1	1F	1	1Ga	1F	1	1		1	
Dusk PLUM	520	1	1		1	1	5			1	1	1	1	1c	1					
Twilight TURQUOISE	512	1H	1	2	1H	1	5J	2	2	1H	1	1H	1	1Jb	1H	1J	1J		1J	
India IVORY	500	1	1	2	1	1	5	2	2	1	1	1	1	1a	1	1	1		1	3

INTERIOR COLOR SYMBOLS:

CONTEMPORARY INTERIOR—(Standard)
1, Ivory-Charcoal
2, Gold-Black
3, Gold-Charcoal
4, Gold-Dark Green
5, Ivory-Black
6, Tan-Copper

CUSTOM-COLORED INTERIOR—(Optional)
A, Yellow-Charcoal
B, Light Green-Dark Green
C, Ivory-Dark Green
D, Light Blue-Dark Blue
E, Ivory-Dark Blue
F, Red-Beige
G, Ivory-Red
H, Light Turquoise-Dark Turquoise
J, Ivory-Dark Turquoise

CONVERTIBLE TOP OPTIONS
a. Ivory or Black
b. Ivory or Black or Tan
c. Ivory or Tan
d. Lt. Blue or Ivory or Tan
e. Lt. Blue or Ivory
f. Tan or Black

14 TWO-TONE COMBINATIONS

India Ivory-
Onyx Black

Onyx Black-
Crocus Yellow

Crocus Yellow-
Laurel Green

Sherwood Green-
Pinecrest Green

India Ivory-
Sherwood Green

India Ivory-
Pinecrest Green

Nassau Blue-
Harbor Blue

India Ivory-
Nassau Blue

India Ivory-
Dusk Plum

India Ivory-
Matador Red

Dune Beige-
Matador Red

Adobe Beige-
Sierra Gold

India Ivory-
Dawn Gray

India Ivory-
Twilight Turquoise

TWO-TONE COLOR STYLING

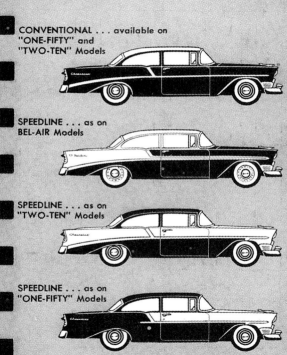

CONVENTIONAL . . . available on
"ONE-FIFTY" and
"TWO-TEN" Models

SPEEDLINE . . . as on
BEL-AIR Models

SPEEDLINE . . . as on
"TWO-TEN" Models

SPEEDLINE . . . as on
"ONE-FIFTY" Models

10 SOLID CAR COLORS

Onyx Black

Crocus Yellow

Sherwood Green

Pinecrest Green

Harbor Blue

Nassau Blue

Matador Red

Dusk Plum

India Ivory

Twilight
Turquoise

202 MODEL-COLOR COMBINATIONS IN 14 EXCITING TWO-TONES

... with standard Contemporary Interior or optional Custom-Colored Interior as indicated in chart. (Refer to first page for symbols)

	Option No.	4-DOOR SEDANS			2-DOOR SEDANS					SPORT MODELS					STATION WAGONS 4-DOOR				2-DOOR	
		BEL AIR SEDAN	"TWO-TEN" SEDAN	"ONE-FIFTY" SEDAN	BEL AIR SEDAN	"TWO-TEN" SEDAN	"TWO-TEN" CLUB COUPE	"ONE-FIFTY" SEDAN	"ONE-FIFTY" UTILITY SEDAN	BEL AIR SPORT SEDAN	"TWO-TEN" SPORT SEDAN	BEL AIR SPORT COUPE	"TWO-TEN" SPORT COUPE	BEL AIR CONVERTIBLE	BEL AIR BEAUVILLE	"TWO-TEN" BEAUVILLE	"TWO-TEN" TOWNSMAN	BEL AIR NOMAD	"TWO-TEN" HANDYMAN	"ONE-FIFTY" HANDYMAN
India IVORY—Onyx BLACK	538	1	1	2	1	1	5	2	2	1	1	1	1	1a	1	1	1	1	1	3
Onyx BLACK—Crocus YELLOW	539	1A	1	2	1A	1	5	2	2	1A	1	1A	1	1Aa	1A	1	1	1A	1	3
Crocus YELLOW—Laurel GREEN	556	1A	1		1A	1	5			1A	1	1A	1	1Aa	1A	1	1	1A	1	
Sherwood GREEN—Pinecrest GREEN	548	1B	1C	2	1B	1C	5C	2	2	1B	1C	1B	1C			1C	1C	1B	1C	4
India IVORY—Sherwood GREEN	528	1B	1C		1B	1C	5C			1B	1C	1B	1C	1Ba		1C	1C	1B	1C	4
India IVORY—Pinecrest GREEN	526	1B	1C	2	1B	1C	5C	2	2	1B	1C	1B	1C	1Ba	1	1C	1C	1B	1C	4
Nassau BLUE—Harbor BLUE	550	1D	1E		1D	1E				1D	1E	1D	1E	1De				1D		
India IVORY—Nassau BLUE	530	1D	1E	2	1D	1E	5	2	2	1D	1E	1D	1E	1De	1	1	1	1D	1	3
India IVORY—Dusk PLUM	534	1	1		1	1	5			1	1	1	1	1a	1	1	1	1	1	
India IVORY—Matador RED	536	1	1	2	1	1	5	2	2		1		1	1Ga		1	1		1	
Dune BEIGE—Matador RED	542									1F		1F			1F				1F	
Adobe BEIGE—Sierra GOLD	541	6			6					6		6		6f	6			6		
India IVORY—Dawn GRAY	555	1	1		1	1				1	1	1	1	1a	1	1	1	1	1	
India IVORY—Twilight TURQUOISE	532	1H	1		1H	1	5J			1H	1	1H	1	1Ja	1H	1J	1J	1H	1J	

BEAUTIFUL, COMFORTABLE, CONVENIENT INTERIORS

Rich, Tasteful Styling

- Contemporary interior or Custom-Colored interior*
- Tailored pattern cloth and vinyl or all-vinyl upholstery*
- All-vinyl sidewalls
- Attractive garnish moldings
- Smartly coved headlining
- Neat carpets or rubber mats*
- Smart chrome hardware and trim*

Wide, Form-Fitting Seats

- Sturdy steel seat frames
- Resilient S-wire springs
- Well-padded cushions, backrests
- Foam-rubber cushions*
- Center-Fold front-seat backs*
- Full-fold rear seat, or folding center and removable rear seats, in station wagons*
- Inclined-Plane front-seat adjustment
- Power-Positioned front seat*
- Built-in or applied armrests*
- Handy loop assist straps*
- Seat belts; shoulder harness*
- Convenient parcel shelf*

Graceful Instrument Panel

- Wraparound contour styling
- Chrome center panel*
- Driver-centered controls and instrument cluster
- Matching radio speaker
- Three accessory radios*
- Central glove compartment with key lock, and light*
- Built-in ashtray
- Pop-out cigaret lighter*
- Electric clock*

Wide, Rear-Opening Doors

- Rotary safety door latches
- Stationary outside handles
- Pushbutton latch releases
- Single key for all car locks
- Automatic lock weathershields
- Swing-out front-door hinges
- Stay-open door checks
- Automatic front-door and rear-door inside light switches*
- Remote control inside handles
- Button-on-sill inside locks
- Keyless door locking

Large Sedan and Coupe Trunk

- Key-turn trunk-lid release
- High-lifting, counterbalanced lid
- Out-of-way lid hinges
- Broad opening; extra-low sill
- Large, rubber-covered floor
- Smooth, washable sidewalls
- Out-of-way spare-wheel mount
- Automatic trunk-lid lock

Extra Utility Sedan Load Space

- Easy access by tilting seatback
- Flat, rubber-covered platform
- Durable composition-board walls

Big Station Wagon Cargo Space

- Large, flat extendible platform
- Linoleum platform surface
- Spare wheel below platform
- Easy access through side doors
- Extra-large rear opening
- High-lifting, two-stop liftgate with telescoping supports
- Double-walled tailgate with cable supports and slam locks
- Dovetail-and-key gate locking

*See text for models in which feature is furnished.

INVITING NEW INTERIORS

(Bel Air Sport Sedan Illustrated)

FASHIONABLE NEW COLOR STYLING

Interior Styling

Comfortable, convenient, beautiful . . . and fashionable aptly describe the interior of each Chevrolet for 1956. For every Chevrolet provides its occupants with all the comforts and conveniences they may want—as *standard*, *optional*, and *accessory* equipment—in a beautiful new interior styled in the latest fashion. In these gorgeous new interiors, striking new designs are offered in rich new fabrics—in new two-color treatments for each series (see color chart). And to make the interiors even more cheerful, the lighter color of each combination predominates.

Contemporary Interiors

Featured in each series is a new *standard Contemporary* color treatment. In Bel Air and "Two-Ten" models, the two colors of this treatment are ivory and charcoal, except for ivory and black in the club coupe. In "One-Fifty" sedans and coupes, they are gold and black, whereas, in the station wagons of this series, they are gold and charcoal, or gold and green depending on the exterior color. As well as being today's most popular colors, these colors were selected because they go well with all of Chevrolet's exciting new exterior colors.

Custom-Colored Interiors

For Bel Airs and "Two-Tens," there also are *optional Custom-Colored* interiors that are color-keyed to the exterior of the selected model. For the Bel Air models, there are combinations of yellow and charcoal; light and dark tones of green, blue, or turquoise; ivory and dark turquoise or red; red and beige; and tan and copper. In the "Two-Ten" series, ivory is combined with dark green, dark blue, or dark turquoise.

Interior Color Selection

Selection of a Contemporary or Custom-Colored interior affects the color alone. The fabrics in which an interior is finished are the same materials in the respective series, with the same high quality and tailoring— no matter what color is selected.

INTERIORS

New Bel Air Styling

New "One-Fifty" Styling

New "Two-Ten" Styling

INTERIORS

MODERN NEW FABRICS

For 1956, the styling of every Chevrolet interior is new—with attractive new treatments in the seat upholstery and body walls, as exemplified on the opposite page. In addition, vinyl is used to a greater extent, in combination with beautiful new pattern cloths individually designed for each series.

Vinyl is a plastic-coated cotton fabric that has been perfected in recent years and has become popular as an upholstery material because of its many fine qualities. One of its features is an attractive surface, that can be dyed any color and can be calendered to simulate leather or textured in other pleasing designs. More important, however, are its great strength, durability, and form retention, its comfortable feeling as a seat covering, and the easiness with which it can be cleaned with soap and water.

Because of these valuable characteristics, vinyl is used extensively in every Chevrolet. In conventional sedans and coupes, it is used in the sidewalls and as seat coverings, except for the cushion cover and lower panel of the backrest cover. In Bel Air sport sedans and sport coupes, and in all station wagons, it is used in the headlining as well. And in the Bel Air convertible, the "Two-Ten" club coupe and Handyman, and the "One-Fifty" Handyman, the entire interior is vinyl.

In the Bel Air sport sedan, sport coupe, and Nomad, and in the "Two-Ten" club coupe, a pleasing effect is obtained by perforating the vinyl headlining, whereas in all station wagons, except the Nomad, the vinyl headlining is not perforated. In all other models, a durable, napped cotton headlining provides a fresh, cool appearance in keeping the overall luxury look of the interiors. Sunshades are covered with the headlining material of the various models. Special vinyl hand-holds are provided on the sunshades of models with napped cloth headlinings to help keep the cloth clean.

Except in those models which have all-vinyl interiors, new pattern cloth for each series is used on each seat cushion cover and the lower panel of each backrest cover. In addition to being beautiful, these materials were developed to withstand fading, wear, and repeated cleanings. Moreover, they have characteristics that contribute to passenger comfort: porosity, or *breathability*, that makes sitting cooler in warm weather and warmer in cool weather, and excellent *slideability* that makes moving into a seat easier.

The new *jacquard-type* pattern cloth for Bel Air conventional sedans resembles striated plywood in appearance, while that for the Bel Air sport sedan, sport coupe, and station wagons has a birchbark pattern. Practically the entire surface of these materials is nylon, giving them sheen and durability as well as sliding ease. The new pattern cloth for the "Two-Ten" sedans and sport coupe features a design of horizontal ribs separated by silver threads and broken up by a regular pattern of one long dash and three short dashes in a darker tone. This also is a nylon-surfaced material. The new pattern cloth for all "One-Fifty" models (except the Handyman) is fabricated of cotton and rayon and features a pattern of small two-tone triangles offset by tiny golden flecks.

The sidewalls of each series are individually styled with attractive panels that are high-lighted in Bel Air and "Two-Ten" models by chrome moldings. All door and sidewall panels are either grained or textured vinyls, providing beauty and washable protection. An interesting styling note in "Two-Ten" and "One-Fifty" models is the repetition of the pattern cloth designs in the vinyl of the central sidewall panels.

For those who wish to preserve the original seat upholstery, there are accessory seat-cushion covers of transparent nylon or sets of seat and backrest covers in plastic, nylon, or fiber—all in a wide choice of colors that go well with Chevrolet interior colors.

Seat Pattern Cloth Qualities

Seat Pattern Cloth Appearance

Sidewall Styling

Accessory Seat Covers

COMFORTABLE SEATS

Chevrolet seats are comfortably wide, providing plenty of room for hips and shoulders. Two front seat types are used. That for four-door models, is a solid structure with an integral backrest. In two-door models, the front-seat backrest is split at the center and each half is hinged so it tilts inward and out of the way as it is folded forward. Rear seats in sedans and coupes are the solid type fitted into the body structure. The single rear seat of the six-passenger station wagons is the fast-folding type. Since both its cushion and backrest fold flat to become part of the load platform, it adds nearly one foot more length to the platform than types in which the cushion is tilted to an upright position.

Seat
Types

The center seat in the nine-passenger station wagons is in two sections that fold separately. The section at the right side accommodates one person; that at the left, two passengers. The rearmost seat of these models also is in two parts—the cushion and the backrest—that are easy to remove individually. To provide ample foot space for this rear seat, the body floor extends back at the same level as for the front and center seats. The platform is in two sections which are hinged at the middle. When the rear seat is to be used, these are *jackknifed* to a vertical position to uncover the foot space and to serve as a support for the seat's backrest.

Entrance to Seats

The front seats in all models and the rear seats of four-door models are right beside the doors. With these seats, entrance is easy. The center-fold front-seat backrests of the two-door models simplify access to the rear seat. To reach the rearmost seat of the nine-passenger station wagons, the right-hand section of the center seat is folded.

In the Bel Air and "Two-Ten" two-door

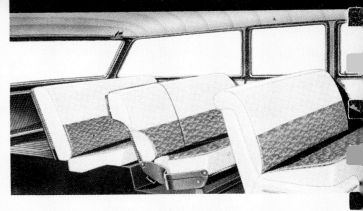

sedans and the "Two-Ten" club coupe, convenient loop-type assist straps facilitate getting in and out of the rear seat.

Assist Straps

All seat frames are sturdy steel structures with resilient S-wire springs that provide lasting uniform body support. Unlike coil springs, they allow plenty of room below the front seat. This provides more footroom and air circulation at the floor level for the greater comfort of rear-seat occupants.

Seat Construction

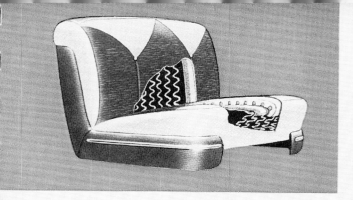

Several layers of heavy jute pads and cotton batts pad the seats. The cotton helps maintain correct contour; the plastic-insulated jute protects the seat coverings from wear. The front-corner foundation of the cushions helps to keep the upholstery wrinkle-free at the corners. The front-seat cushions of the Bel Air and "Two-Ten" models and the rear-seat cushions of Bel Air sedans, coupes, convertible, and Nomad also have an extra-deep layer of foam rubber to assure relaxing easy-chair comfort.

Seat Padding

Accessory seat belts and belt and shoulder harness combinations are available for all 1956 models. Exceeding the specifications of the Civil Aeronautics Authority for aircraft seat belts, they are securely anchored to minimize the possibility of injury in the event of accidents.

Seat Belts

Armrests are standard in Bel Air and "Two-Ten" models and are available as accessories in the "One-Fifty" series (see chart at end of section). They come in two styles: the smart built-in type used in more expensive cars and the attractive applied type that features a sturdy plastic base. All are comfortably padded with foam rubber and are surfaced with durable, washable vinyl. In addition, those on the doors are the doorpull type, with handgrips that facilitate door closing.

Armrests

All window regulators and door control levers are shaped and located for easiest operation. Their low hubs place them close to the sidewalls so they are not likely to catch on clothing. Designed by master craftsmen and finished in chrome with black plastic knobs, they reflect the best taste.

Door Hardware

A spring-assisted inclined-plane adjustment permits the front seat to be moved forward and up, or backward and down, with pushbutton ease. The seat rises and tilts forward as it is moved ahead so the driver sits more erectly. The adjustment range is large (4.4"), so nearly every driver is assured of a comfortable driving position. The chrome pushbutton control is easily reached without stooping or fumbling. An electric-power control (Option 397) for Bel Air and "Two-Ten" sedans and coupes, adjusts the seat automatically at the touch of a finger.

Front-Seat Adjustment

Floor coverings for 1956 include: colored, nylon-rayon pile carpeting in Bel Airs and the "Two-Ten" club coupe; colored rubber mats, in "Two-Tens," which are coated with vinyl to prevent fading of the color; and black rubber mats in "One-Fifty" models. Accessory rubber mats for individual seat occupants come in many colors and two types: one covers the flat portion of the floor; one covers the floor of the front compartment and extends up on the toepan.

Floor Coverings

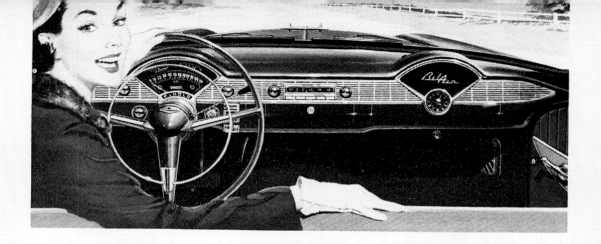

BEAUTIFUL, PRACTICAL INSTRUMENT PANELS

Quick to take the eye is the smart modern design of the instrument panel that follows the broad graceful contour of the panoramic windshield. And only a second glance is required to recognize the practicality em-

bodied in its design. The basic instrument panel features a quadrant-shaped instrument cluster directly in front of the driver with a matching radio speaker grille ahead of the front-seat passenger. The graceful hoods of

these quadrants prevent the reflection of instrument and clock lights in the windshield. Convenient to both the driver and passenger is the central glove compartment. The instrument cluster houses all instruments where the driver can see them fast and all controls are grouped around the cluster within quick, easy reach of his hands.

A different appearance is given to the instrument panel of each series by an individual chrome and paint treatment. In Bel Air models, the entire panel is one color with a distinctive chrome molding on the central section, chrome quadrant frames and control knobs, and a gold-plated *Bel Air* on the radio speaker grille. The panel of the

"Two-Tens" is like that of the Bel Airs except that the central section is painted ivory and a chrome *Chevrolet* is on the radio speaker grille. The basic color of these two panels depends on the car color. In the "One-Fifty" models, the upper section of the panel is black or green, depending on the car's exterior color. The remainder of the panel is beige, a color which is continued in the steering wheel, its column and the control levers on the column. Chrome decoration is confined to the quadrant frames, the *Chevrolet* on the radio speaker grille, the ignition switch, and the glove compartment lock. The control knobs are black plastic.

Instruments

The instrument cluster is high on the instrument panel where it is fully visible through the steering wheel. Its quadrant shape permits the speedometer to be made sweepingly large for split-second scanning. Above it are the accurate electrically operated engine temperature and gasoline gauges. Below it are the odometer, indicating miles travelled, and the transmission selector indicator of Powerglide-equipped models. The large white numerals and letters of these indicators stand out sharply on a black background. At night they are illuminated by a soft white indirect lighting that may be adjusted to suit driving conditions or even turned off. The same type of numerals and lighting are features of the handsome electric clock of Bel Air models and the accessory radio dial. For 1956, an added fuse protects the instrument panel light circuit.

Warning Lights

On the body of the instrument cluster are warning lights that contribute to driving safety and convenience. If the country headlight beams are on, if the oil pressure is low, or if the generator output drops below normal, one of three red lights gleams a warning. When the turn signal is used, a green arrow at the left of the cluster, or one at the right, flashes intermittently to indicate the direction of the turn. To guard against driving with the parking brakes applied, an accessory red warning signal, under the instrument panel, lights automatically when the ignition is turned on, and flashes until the brakes are released.

INSTRUMENT PANEL CONVENIENCES

Glove Compartment

Both driver and passenger benefit from having the glove compartment in the center of the panel, where it is most accessible. The large, fully lined compartment slants downward so its contents won't fall out when the door is opened. Moreover, the door opens level to serve as a handy shelf. Two indentations on this shelf are shaped to hold cups for roadside snacks. The pushbutton keylock is standard equipment. In Bel Air and "Two-Ten" models, the glove compartment is lighted automatically when its door is opened. The same light may be obtained as an accessory in "One-Fifty" models.

Clock

The electric clock used in all Bel Airs is also available as an accessory in "Two-Ten" and "One-Fifty" models. Mounted below the radio speaker grille, it is a self-starting precision timepiece with a sapphire-jeweled movement and convenient hand-set knob.

In every Chevrolet, a tilting, bin-type ashtray is convenient to the driver's right hand. Concealed in the instrument panel, it opens with a gentle push at its lower edge.

Ashtrays

Rearseat ashtrays also are provided in Bel Air and "Two-Ten" sedans and coupes. In the two-door sedans and coupes of these series, box-like ashtrays with snap covers are built in the rear-seat armrests; in the four-door sedans, a tilting ashtray is inset in the back of the front seat. All ashtrays have snuffers and may be lifted out for cleaning.

Cigaret Lighter

Above and to the left of the ashtray on the instrument panel of Bel Air and "Two-Ten" models is a handy electric pop-out cigaret lighter that also is available as an accessory in "One-Fifty" models. A shield around its element catches burning tobacco fragments so they won't burn clothing.

Shaver

A boon to the man who must travel early and late is the accessory four-head electric shaver that plugs into the cigaret-lighter socket. It operates on twelve volts D.C. in the car and on 110 volts A.C. at home.

An accessory illuminated compass, that can be mounted on top of the instrument panel center, serves as a convenient guide when travelling by day or night.

The illuminated dial and handy controls of any of the accessory radios are centered on the instrument panel above the glove compartment. To suit every budget, Chevrolet offers three radios as accessories.

For the greatest convenience, there is an ultra-modern eight-tube (with rectifier) receiver, with pushbuttons that may be set to the owner's five favorite local stations, and a signal-seeking feature that is particularly convenient for travelers. When a bar above the dial is pressed repeatedly, the tuner accurately tunes in—in frequency sequence —the stations of the locality in which the car is traveling.

In addition, there are a modern super-heterodyne seven-tube (with rectifier) receiver operated by five pushbuttons, and a six-tube (with rectifier) hand-tuned receiver.

Each radio is furnished with a super-sensitive chrome-plated antenna that is mounted on the right front fender near the windshield. Matched to all three radios, it gives equally good performance in the city or open country. Tension springs keep its sections from rattling. When telescoped, it projects only a short distance above the fender top. For those who prefer the antenna to be mounted at the rear of the car, an accessory adapter permits the antenna to be mounted on the right rear fender top.

A large (6″ x 9″) accessory radio speaker can be mounted beneath the parcel shelf of sedans and coupes (except the convertible). Controlled by a switch on the instrument panel, it can be used in combination with the instrument panel speaker to give excellent tone quality and tone distribution throughout the car for greater enjoyment.

A handy, chrome-plated tissue dispenser, designed to hold a standard size box of tissues, is also obtainable as an accessory. It mounts directly below the radio speaker grille on the instrument panel and swivels out, making the tissues readily available.

DRIVER-CENTERED CONTROLS

EASY-TO READ INSTRUMENTS

- All instruments clustered ahead of driver
- Extra-large speedometer, with odometer
- Electric gasoline and temperature gauges
- Red generator-charge, oil-pressure and country-beam warning lights
- Green right and left turn-signal lights
- Powerglide* selector dial in cluster
- Large, well-lighted letters and figures
- Instrument light intensity control

HANDY KNOBS AND SWITCHES

- Master light switch controlling all lights
- Windshield-wiper and washer* controls
- Lighted key-turn ignition-starter switch
- Individual knobs for cowl side ventilators
- Radio, heater, and air-conditioner controls*
- Heater and air-conditioner control lights*

CONVENIENT HANDLES AND PEDALS

- Man-size, three- or two-spoke* deep-hub steering wheel; concentric steering column
- Full-circle horn ring or large horn button*
- Steering-column transmission control lever
- Steering-column turn-signal control lever
- Parking brake and overdrive* pull-handles
- Suspended clutch* and brake pedals
- Sure-grip rubber pedal pads
- Headlight-beam foot switch

*—See text for models in which feature is furnished.

CONVENIENT DRIVING CONTROLS

Hand Controls

Within easy reach around the instrument cluster on the instrument panel are the convenient hand controls: the main light switch, the windshield wiper control, the key-turn ignition-starter switch, and the control panel for the accessory heater or air conditioner. There is no choke control because the choke is automatic on *every* Chevrolet. All of these controls are clearly labelled. In addition, the keyhole of the ignition-starter switch is lighted for easy key insertion at night and the heater or air-conditioner control panel is indirectly illuminated.

Starter-Ignition Switch

A feature of considerable convenience is the four-position operation of the ignition-starter switch: *locked-off*, *unlocked-off*, *on*, and *start*. When the car is left in a parking lot, the switch can be left in the *unlocked-off* position, which permits the attendant to start the car without the key. Consequently the driver can take the key with him so the contents of his locked glove compartment and trunk will be safer. Chevrolet's famous positive-shift starter is activated by turning either the integral knob of the switch or the inserted key to *start*. When released, the switch automatically returns to *on*.

Steering Wheels

Chevrolet steering wheels are all the deep-hub type, with three spokes in Bel Air models and two spokes in "Two-Ten" and "One-Fifty" models. The hubs of these wheels are deeply recessed to keep them out of the way in the event of accidents in which the steering wheel may be bent. In addition, they are out of the vision range of the instruments. Bel Air models have a gold-plated steering wheel hub emblem and a full-circle chrome horn-blowing ring. "Two-Ten" models have the same ring but the emblem is chrome-plated. The hub of the "One-Fifty" steering wheel is a large horn button with an attractive chrome emblem.

In the interest of greater safety, turn-signals are now standard in every Chevrolet. The lever controls for the transmission and the turn signals are just below the steering wheel for fingertip operation. All their mechanism is neatly concealed in the concentric steering column. And their knobs are black plastic to keep them looking clean longer.

Control Levers

Controls for the parking brakes and the optional overdrive transmission are located at the sides of the steering column just below the instrument panel. Both are the pullout type with T-shaped handles that are easy to grasp for a straight-back pull.

Pull Handles

Each pedal is surfaced with a large grooved rubber foot pad to assure a firm, comfortable foot grip. Suspended brake and clutch pedals allow more footroom and eliminate holes in the toepan for better sealing. The pedal linkages to the clutch, brake, and carburetor are located high, to protect them from road dirt, and are designed to avoid the transmission of road shocks and engine vibrations to the driver's feet.

Pedals

DOORS THAT STAY CLOSED

Chevrolet doorways are large with low sills. Around the inner edge of each doorway, a *windlace* serves as a second seal, in addition to that on the door itself. Made of sponge rubber encased in fabric, it also helps prevent passengers from bruising themselves when getting in and out. Attractive plates of etched aluminum protect the sills.

The doors are hinged at the front for safety and open wide for easy entrance. Offset hinges actually move the front doors out of the way to increase entrance room. Positive checks hold the doors wide open until they are shut intentionally. Rotary safety latches permit the doors to close more easily and quietly, and hold them securely shut. Even if a door is not completely closed, it will not open, because teeth of the rotary latch act as safety catches. New for 1956, special latch design prevents unintentional opening of closed doors under almost every conceivable circumstance.

There's no fumbling with keys when unlocking a door, trunk, or endgate, because one key operates all car locks. The lock weather seals don't have to be pushed aside by hand in order to insert the key. Instead, simple insertion or removal of the key automatically causes the seal to uncover or cover the keyhole. The car key is numbered so the owner can order duplicates. The number is on a tab that is removable so thieves cannot identify the key by its number. The pushbutton lock releases of all doors are shielded from snow and drippings by the solidly mounted door handles, to assure that the doors will open easily at all times.

Button-on-sill latches are provided inside every door and those on rear doors are *baby-proof*—the doors won't open as long as the buttons are down. When all buttons are down, the car can be locked from outside, without the key, simply by pushing the outside pushbutton in, as the last door is shut.

SPACIOUS
LUGGAGE COMPARTMENTS

Just a twist of the key, and the trunk lid of sedans and coupes is immediately released. It lifts high so no one will strike his head against it when loading the trunk. Efficient counterbalancing makes raising the lid a smooth one-finger operation. The concealed, full-travel hinges are out of the way so they can't interfere with or damage luggage. The sill is exceptionally low (about one inch above the floor) and the opening is unusually broad—providing easy loading without strain. The trunk itself is spacious, with a 20-cubic-foot capacity (17 cubic feet in the convertible). A neat durable black rubber mat covers its floor. The metal sidewalls are neatly painted; the front wall is durable black composition board. The spare wheel is inclined in a well at the right. Both the wheel and jack are clamped in place so they don't rattle. The lid lowers with ease and locks automatically, without slamming, when closed.

Sedan and Coupe Trunks

INTERIORS

To increase trunk space and give the car an extra-long sports car look, a combination of an outside wheel carrier and a special rear bumper is available as an accessory for all sedans and coupes. The wheel, with its metal cover, is mounted vertically behind the rear deck within an offset in the bumper. For access to the trunk, it can be easily tilted so it is out of the way.

Continental Wheel Carrier

The extra load compartment behind the front seat of the utility sedan is easily reached by folding either front-seat backrest. In harmony with this model's gold-trimmed interior, the whole compartment is black. The seat-back is finished with tough washable vinyl; the sidewalls and rearwall are rugged composition board. The flat, elevated floor is surfaced with a durable black rubber mat. The load compartment has 31-cubic-foot capacity from floor to window sills, in addition to 20 cubic feet of trunk space. Also, as in all Chevrolet sedans and coupes except the convertible, there is a broad parcel shelf beneath the rear window.

Utility Sedan Load Compartment

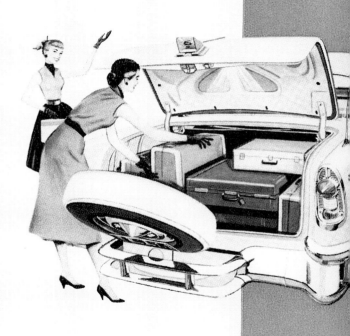

BIG STATION WAGON CARGO COMPARTMENTS

Platform

In all station wagons, the large steel platform is lengthened by folding the seat behind the driver's seat and is further extended by lowering the tailgate. Durable ribbed linoleum covers this entire surface, including the floor, the exposed surfaces of the folded seat, and the lowered tailgate. Black or dark green in "One-Fifty" models and colored in all others, the linoleum is edged with protective chrome at the front and rear of the platform and around the exposed surfaces of the folded seat. The spare wheel, in its well below the platform, is reached by lifting out a section of the platform.

Side Loading

The rear side doors of four-door models give direct access to the load space; in two-door models, curbside loading is made possible by the center-folding front-seat backrests.

The double-walled tailgate is supported by two sturdy hinges and stout steel cables at the sides. The cables hold the gate at an angle that tends to prevent the cargo from sliding out. They are provided with springs that keep the cables taut, so they won't rattle, and rewind the cables while the gate is being closed. Slam latches at the sides are operated by a central outside chrome T-handle, with an integral weather-protected keylock. A dovetail on the gate's top engages a wedge to lock the liftgate. The box-sectioned liftgate, framing the rear window, lifts to two positions on concealed hinges and is held up by self-latching telescoping chrome supports. To close the gate, releases at the supports are disengaged and the gate is lifted slightly before lowering.

Endgates

In Bel Air station wagons, vinyl covers the sidewalls of the load compartment as well as the doors. Also, the spare wheel well and its cover are edged with chrome. Special features of the Bel Air Nomad include chrome roof bows and window garnish moldings and an additional switch, at the tailgate, that operates the two inside lights.

Bel Air Features

MODEL STANDARD EQUIPMENT COMPARISON	4-DOOR SEDANS			2-DOOR SEDANS					SPORT MODELS					STATION WAGON 4-DOOR			2-DOOR		
	BEL AIR SEDAN	"TWO-TEN" SEDAN	"ONE-FIFTY" SEDAN	BEL AIR SEDAN	"TWO-TEN" SEDAN	"TWO-TEN" CLUB COUPE	"ONE-FIFTY" SEDAN	"ONE-FIFTY" UTILITY SEDAN	BEL AIR SPORT SEDAN	"TWO-TEN" SPORT SEDAN	BEL AIR SPORT COUPE	"TWO-TEN" SPORT COUPE	BEL AIR CONVERTIBLE	BEL AIR BEAUVILLE	"TWO-TEN" BEAUVILLE	"TWO-TEN" TOWNSMAN	BEL AIR NOMAD	"TWO-TEN" HANDYMAN	"ONE-FIFTY" HANDYMAN
Armrests, Front (Built-in [B] or applied [A])	B	A	E	B	A	A	E	E	B	A	B	A	B	B	A	A	B	A	E
Armrests, Rear (Built-in [B] or applied [A])	B	A	E	A	A	A	E		B	A	B	B	B						
Ashtray, Instrument panel	1	1	1	1	1	1	1	1	1	1	1	1	1	1	1	1	1	1	1
Ashtray, Rear	1	1		2	2	2			1	1	2	2	2						
Assist straps				2	2	2													
Carpets [C] or rubber floor mats [M]	C	M	M	C	M	C	M	M	C	M	C	M	C	M	M	M	C	M	M
Cigaret lighter	1	1	E	1	1	1	E	E	1	1	1	1	1	1	1	1	1	1	E
Clock, Electric	1	E	E	1	E	E	E	E	1	E	1	E	1	1	E	E	1	E	E
Coat hooks	2	2		2	2	2			2	2	2	2		2	2	2	2	2	
Glove compartment automatic light	1	1	E	1	1	1	E	E	1	1	1	1	1	1	1	1	1	1	E
Glove compartment key lock	1	1	1	1	1	1	1	1	1	1	1	1	1	1	1	1	1	1	1
Horn ring [R] or button [B]	R	R	B	R	R	R	B	B	R	R	R	R	R	R	R	R	R	R	B

E—Available at extra cost.

INTERIORS

	4-DOOR SEDANS			2-DOOR SEDANS					SPORT MODELS					STATION WAGONS 4-DOOR				STATION WAGONS 2-DOOR	
	BEL AIR SEDAN	"TWO-TEN" SEDAN	"ONE-FIFTY" SEDAN	BEL AIR SEDAN	"TWO-TEN" SEDAN	"TWO-TEN" CLUB COUPE	"ONE-FIFTY" SEDAN	"ONE-FIFTY" UTILITY SEDAN	BEL AIR SPORT SEDAN	"TWO-TEN" SPORT SEDAN	BEL AIR SPORT COUPE	"TWO-TEN" SPORT COUPE	BEL AIR CONVERTIBLE	BEL AIR BEAUVILLE	"TWO-TEN" BEAUVILLE	"TWO-TEN" TOWNSMAN	BEL AIR NOMAD	"TWO-TEN" HANDYMAN	"ONE-FIFTY" HANDYMAN
Light automatic door switches, Inside	4	2		2	2	2			4	2	2	2	2	4	2	2	2	2	
Light, Inside	1	1	1	1	1	1	1	1	1	1	1	1	2	1	1	1	2	1	1
Locks, Car key (On both front doors)	2	2	2	2	2	2	2	2	2	2	2	2	2	2	2	2	2	2	2
Parcel shelf	1	1	1	1	1	1	1	1	1	1	1	1							
Rearview mirror, Inside	1	1	1	1	1	1	1	1	1	1	1	1	1	1	1	1	1	1	1
Seat cushion pad, Foam-rubber front	1	1		1	1	1			1	1	1	1	1	1	1	1	1	1	
Seat cushion pad, Foam-rubber rear	1			1					1		1		1				1		
Steering wheel, Three- or two-spoke	3	2	2	3	2	2	2	2	3	2	3	2	3	3	2	2	3	2	2
Sunshade, Left-side	1	1	1	1	1	1	1	1	1	1	1	1	1	1	1	1	1	1	1
Sunshade, Right-side	1	1	E	1	1	1	E	E	1	1	1	1	1	1	1	1	1	1	E
Ventipane crank regulators, Front	2	2	2	2	2	2	2	2	2	2	2	2	2	2	2	2	2	2	2
Windshield wipers, Vacuum	2	2	2	2	2	2	2	2	2	2	2	2	2	2	2	2	2	2	2

E-Available at extra cost.
INTERIORS

Superior Vision

- Broad Panoramic windshield
- Wide Vista rear window
- Four-Fender visibility
- Extra-large side windows
- Separate rear-quarter windows in four-door sedans
- Wraparound rear-quarter windows in station wagons
- High-quality safety glass
- E-Z-Eye tinted safety glass*

Complete Driving Vision Aids

- Full-width windshield defrosting provision
- Dual windshield wipers
- Optional electric wipers*
- Accessory windshield washer*
- Fully adjustable sunshades
- Accessory outside sun visor*
- Inside rearview mirror; also accessory prismatic-type*
- Accessory outside mirrors*

*—Accessory or optional equipment

All Weather Comfort

- Full sealing and insulation
- High-Level air intake with individual outlet controls
- Crank-operated ventipanes
- Crank-operated side windows
- Power-Controlled side windows*
- Two accessory heaters*
- Air conditioning by Frigidaire*
- Built-in ventilator, heater and air-conditioner controls*

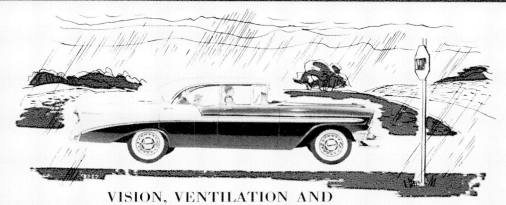

VISION, VENTILATION AND
WEATHER CONTROL
. . . *for safer, healthier driving*
in *any* *weather!*

COMPLETE WEATHER PROTECTION

In the 1956 Chevrolet, both the driver and passengers can enjoy the safest, most comfortable transportation, despite the weather. Rain, snow, sun glare, heat, and cold present no serious problems—because, in addition to the most up-to-date *standard* weather-defeating features, Chevrolet makes available a variety of *accessory* and *optional* equipment that was developed to defeat every kind of adverse weather condition effectively. This permits a Chevrolet buyer to select the most suitable equipment to deal with the weather prevailing in the part of the country in which he lives. Thus he is relieved of buying any weatherizing aid that is unnecessary for his particular needs.

Windshield Vision

The big one-piece panoramic windshield curves in a continuous sweep into the body sides, where it meets the vertical pillars that set back beyond the driver's normal range of vision. In profile, it carries high into the top to give an improved view of overhead traffic lights. In conventional models, the windshield height is $17\frac{1}{2}$ inches. Even though the sport models and Nomad are up to $1\frac{1}{2}$ inches lower in overall height, their windshield is only $\frac{3}{4}$-inch less tall than that of the conventional models. For 1956, Chevrolet has taken every precaution to maintain this sweep-sight windshield vision that is so important to safe driving.

Windshield Defrosting

Under cold weather conditions, heated air from the accessory heater or air conditioner can be directed across the full width of the windshield to clear the glass of ice, snow, and frost. Because of important improvements, defrosting is three times more efficient for 1956.

Windshield Wipers and Washers

Two vacuum-operated windshield wipers, controlled by a turn knob at the left of the steering column, are standard on every model. Two-speed electric wipers (Option 320) provide constant speed action independent of the engine and clear nearly 25 percent more area than the standard wipers. Accessory wiper blades have rubber hoods that flex to flake off ice and snow. An accessory vacuum-operated washer sprays liquid on the windshield at the push of a button inset in the wiper control knob. For automatic cleaning, there is a foot-operated accessory washer-wiper that sprays water, starts the blades, cleans the glass, and stops the blades.

Windshield Sunshades

Two sunshades are standard in Bel Air and "Two-Ten" models. Although only one for the driver is provided in "One-Fifty" models, a second is available as an accessory. All sunshades can be swivelled up and down to shield the driver's eyes and can be moved

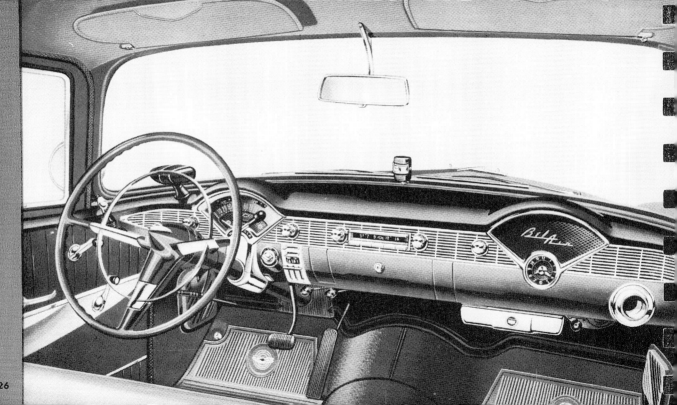

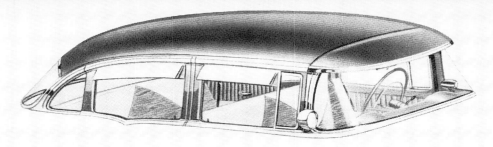

from the windshield to the side windows. Except in the convertible, the lowered shades can be moved laterally on their shafts to meet behind the rearview mirror, thus restricting glare across the windshield. A make-up mirror, which clips to the back of either sunshade, is obtainable as an accessory.

Sunshade Vanity Mirror

E-Z-Eye green-tinted safety glass (Option 398) reduces glare through all windows and keeps the car cooler in hot weather. An accessory glare shield of light green plastic that filters out 80 per cent of sunglare and bright lights can be fitted across the top of the windshield inside the glass.

Tinted Glass and Glare Shield

An accessory sun visor—chrome-edged and painted to match or contrast with the colors of the car—can be mounted above the windshield of all Turret Top models. Similar shields of stainless steel are available as accessories for the side windows of the conventional sedans and club coupe. They permit opening the windows while it's raining.

Outside Sun Visor

A prismatic traffic light viewer, that mounts on top of the instrument panel, also is available as an accessory. It shows traffic lights in their true colors when direct view of the lights through the windshield is blocked.

Traffic Light Viewer

WEATHERIZING

WIDE VISTA REAR VISION

Rear
Window
Vision

Full wraparound rear windows in all Chevrolet sedans, sport coupes and the club coupe provide more *looking out* area and allow the driver of a following car to see completely through a Chevrolet so that he may observe traffic changes ahead. Similar results are obtained with the large vinyl-plastic rear window in the convertible top and the large liftgate window and wraparound rear-quarter windows of the station wagons.

Inside
Rearview
Mirrors

In all models, a universally adjustable rearview mirror is mounted inside above the center of the windshield. It may be set at any angle, and its offset mounting even permits it to be lowered to suit shorter persons. An inside, nonglare, prismatic accessory mirror may be substituted for the standard one. A flip of a tab on its lower edge changes the mirror from clearview daytime vision to glareproof nighttime vision.

An accessory outside mirror mounts on the door to give a good view of cars coming from behind—for safety when moving out of a parking space or when moving out of a traffic lane to pass other cars. There is also an accessory outside mirror that can be adjusted from inside the car. An outside rearview mirror, built into the accessory sealed-beam spotlight, also can be adjusted from the inside. All outside mirrors are adjustable to any angle and are designed to fit either side of the car so they may be used in pairs.

Outside
Rearview
Mirrors

Chevrolet occupants are well protected from glass breakage and vagaries of the climate.

Every window pane is high-quality safety glass. Two kinds are used, depending on the shape and size of the window. The solid type breaks only under terrific impact into small, blunt-edged, harmless chunks. The laminated type consists of a sandwich of two glass panes that are bonded together by tough, transparent, blister-proof plastic. This type can be crushed, rolled, and warped, but the glass particles still will adhere to the plastic.

Glass Safety Features

Every window pane, door, or rear closure is tightly sealed to keep out wind, cold, rain, and dust. All stationary windows are solidly sealed in rubber. Compressed rubber seals are used around the ventipanes. Other windows that open slide in rubber-backed, fabric-lined, glass-run channels. Vertically opening windows have special seals at their sills, both inside and outside the glass. To assure a

Body Sealing

tight seal when the doors are closed, in addition to *windlace*, rubber seals are retained on the doors by rubber cement and by many metal clips which prevent the seals from coming loose and dangling. Rubber seals and *windlace* also seal the endgates of the station wagons. In the other models, rubber around the trunk opening protects the contents of the trunk. The floor has no holes through which water and dirt might enter.

Chevrolet occupants enjoy complete, all-round body insulation. Heavy insulating materials under the roof, on the floor below the carpets or mats, in the doors and body sidewalls, below the mat on the trunk floor and under the trunk lid, and also in the wheelhouses not only insulate against heat and cold but also minimize annoying road sounds. In addition, thick insulation on the dash and heavy insulating boards on the cowl sides also serve to deaden engine sounds.

Body Insulation

CONTROLLED HEALTHFUL VENTILATION

All Chevrolets provide healthful ventilation whether the windows are opened or closed.

Window Crank Regulators

All windows that open, including the front-door ventipanes, are controlled by easy-turning positive-acting crank regulators. All crank-operated windows open fully. Crank-operation of the pivoting, chrome-edged, rectangular ventipanes eliminates tugging to introduce draft-free air into the car, or to reverse them to scoop in great quantities of air. The spring-loaded, sliding-bolt latches of the ventipanes guard against illegal entry.

Side Window Types

The conventional four-door sedans have crank-operated ventipanes and door windows and stationary rear-quarter windows. Two-door sedans, sport sedans, sport coupes, club coupe, and convertible have crank-operated ventipanes, door windows, and rear-quarter windows. Rear-quarter windows in the utility sedan are stationary. In all station wagons, there are crank-operated ventipanes and door windows, with stationary wrap-around rear-quarter windows. The Nomad has sliding middle window panes. The "Two-Ten" Handyman has crank-operated middle panes. In the "One-Fifty" Handyman, the middle panes are stationary.

Power Controlled Windows

Electric-power control (Option 426) is available for the side windows of the Bel Air and "Two-Ten" models. Besides a master control at the driver's window, there are individual controls for each window.

High-Level Ventilation

To provide ventilation with the windows open or closed, Chevrolet's High-Level ventilation system draws outside air through five banks of louvers that span the cowl just below the windshield. This high-level air intake maintains a generous supply of cleaner, cooler air because it is located above low-lying road dust and annoying road fumes.

With Chevrolet's field-exclusive High-Level ventilation system, before any air enters the car interior, it flows into a large *plenum chamber* that is formed by the double walls of the cowl. Any water in the air is expelled to the ground through drains in the chamber floor. Drainage capacity is 14 gallons of water per minute.

The clean, dry air then enters the interior of the car through two large outlets that are located in the cowl side panels, in each side of the body. The outlets are individually controlled by convenient push-pull knobs at the instrument panel ends. The design and placement of the outlets allow a large volume of air to circulate throughout the interior.

Air circulation is aided by the front-door ventipanes. When the ventipanes are opened, they permit stale air to be drawn outside while controlled outside air is constantly provided by the two outlets to keep the driver and passengers more comfortable and alert.

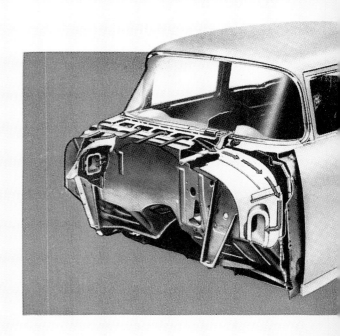

ALL-WEATHER COMFORT CONTROL

Windshield Defroster

For improved driving vision and greater driving safety in inclement weather, the defroster of Chevrolet's two heaters, and the air conditioner as well, is designed to clear the full width of the windshield 300 percent more efficiently than the previous defroster.

Recirculating Heater

The accessory recirculating heater, controlled by two knobs on the instrument panel, heats the air within the car and keeps it circulating. One knob controls the temperature; the second controls the defroster. A high-speed blower blows the air through the heater or defroster outlets.

De Luxe Heater

The accessory De Luxe heater heats and circulates inside air, or outside air it draws from the *plenum chamber*. It can change the air inside the car about once every minute. When operated alone, its high-speed blower, like an electric fan, makes the interior feel cooler. All controls are in a lighted, chrome panel beside the ignition switch on the instrument panel.

Frigidaire Air Conditioning

Chevrolet's air conditioning (accessory or Option 450 for V8 models except the convertible) provides controlled heating, cooling, and dehumidifying for all-weather comfort. For convenient serviceability, all its major components are in the engine compartment, leaving the trunk space free for luggage. Air from the *plenum chamber* enters the car, dehumidified and at the desired temperature, through any combination of outlets: the floor distributor, adjustable air-liner-type nozzles (located at the ends of the instrument panel where both driver and passenger can control the amount and direction of the air), and the defroster slots. No matter what the weather, all occupants are comfortable. Windows stay closed, keeping out bugs, dust, and annoying sounds. Traffic is less tiresome, long trips seem shorter, and driver and passengers arrive feeling fresh and neat. The illuminated controls are located on the instrument panel ahead of the driver's right hand.

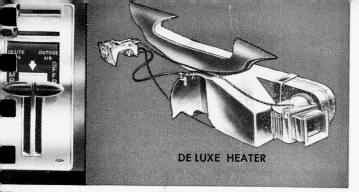

DE LUXE HEATER

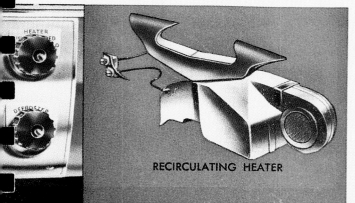

RECIRCULATING HEATER

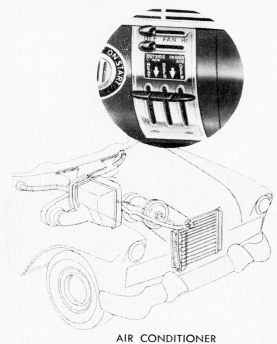

AIR CONDITIONER

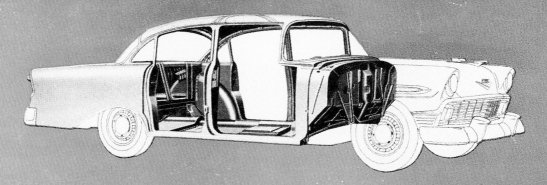

FISHER UNISTEEL BODY CONSTRUCTION

- All-steel, all-welded unit construction
- Solid one-piece Turret Top . . . reinforced at sides, ends, and across its middle
- Heavily ribbed full-length floor . . . reinforced by ladder of box-sectioned beams
- Unitized double-walled body sides
- Double-walled doors
- Double-walled cowl . . . reinforced by integral dash and instrument panels

- Box-sectioned door and window pillars
- Mid-body frame . . . comprised of roof bow, door pillars, and floor crossbeam*
- Rigid rear-quarter brace . . . integrated seat-back support and parcel shelf*
- Reinforced trunk lid; double-walled gates*
- Extra-rigid body-to-frame dash legs
- Thorough rust-preventive treatment
- Rubber-cushioned body-to-frame mounting*

*—See text for models in which feature is furnished

STRUCTURE

Unitized Front-End Structure

- Rigid one-piece-skirt fender construction
- Rigid-beam fender-to-fender front integration
- Solid, bolted, fender-to-cowl rear integration
- Reinforced single-panel hood
- Stabilized front-end mounting

Extra-Rigid Frame and Bumpers

- Box-Girder chassis frame with box-section siderails and front crossmember
- Sturdy, wraparound bumpers, solidly mounted to frame ends and corner-braced to frame siderails

SOLID CONSTRUCTION FOR SAFETY AND SILENCE
. . . and years of trouble-free service!

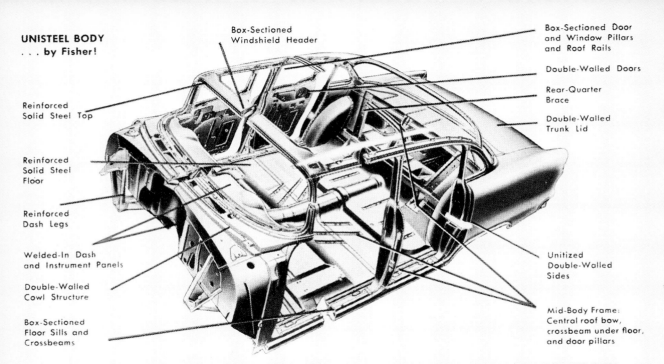

UNISTEEL BODY
. . . by Fisher!

Box-Sectioned
Windshield Header

Box-Sectioned Door
and Window Pillars
and Roof Rails

Double-Walled Doors

Rear-Quarter
Brace

Reinforced
Solid Steel Top

Double-Walled
Trunk Lid

Reinforced
Solid Steel
Floor

Reinforced
Dash Legs

Welded-In Dash
and Instrument Panels

Unitized
Double-Walled
Sides

Double-Walled
Cowl Structure

Box-Sectioned
Floor Sills and
Crossbeams

Mid-Body Frame:
Central roof bow,
crossbeam under floor,
and door pillars

STURDY STEEL COMPONENTS FUSED INTO A SOLID SINGLE STRUCTURE!

STRUCTURE

UNISTEEL BODY CONSTRUCTION

Peace of mind is "standard equipment" in a Chevrolet. For there is a real sense of security in knowing that this car has been engineered for utmost safety—with built-in protection in a solid structural design that features closely integrated body and chassis units.

The body of a car is considered as two parts separated by the dash panel. That part ahead of the dash is the *front-end structure;* that behind the dash is the *body structure.* The body structure of every Chevrolet is of all-steel, all-welded construction—with all components fused into a solid, substantial unit with double walls of steel.

The one-piece all-steel Turret Top of all closed models is rigidly reinforced by box-sections at its sides and ends and is strengthened by a central bow (two in conventional station wagons) that gives maximum bracing from side to side. The pillars that join the top to the base of the body are all rigid beams of reinforced box section—strong but

narrow so they don't impair vision. Integral drip moldings extending the length of the sides (and over the station wagon gates) quickly drain water from the top so it won't drip on persons entering or leaving the car.

The full-length, all-steel floor, or *underbody,* with integral toepan and embossed rear-seat footrest, is made from heavy-gauge steel that's ribbed to make it stiffer. It is further strengthened by box-sectioned sills and crossbeams—like basement beams in a house. In this reinforcement, four U-shaped channel crossbeams are welded under the floor to form box sections with the floor. Use of suspended pedals eliminates openings in the floor for better body sealing. The spare wheel wells in all models are formed integral with the floor. In the nine-passenger station wagons, the floor is extended back at the same level as for the front and center seats to provide generous footroom for the passengers in the rearmost seat.

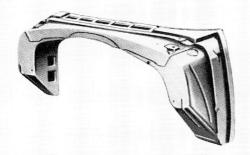

Designed with double walls to form the plenum chamber for the ventilation system, the cowl is actually two cowls—one within the other. Reinforced at its front and rear by the welded-in dash and instrument panels, it spans the frame, giving a firm arch-type support to the front of the body. Rigid dash legs at the front of the cowl help maintain accurate alignment of the body and chassis frame, and are located to reduce transmission of vibration and road shock to the body.

Double-Walled Cowl

Dash-to-Frame Braces

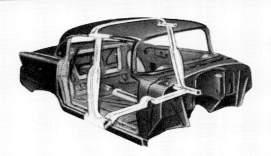

In all conventional sedans and coupes and the station wagons, a rugged structure girds the center of the body. The central roof bow ties in with the door pillars; the pillars in turn are strengthened by a floor crossbeam to complete a sturdy mid-body frame.

In the new four-door hardtop sport sedans, the hinge pillars of the rear doors do not extend above the belt line. To add the necessary rigidity, each of these *stub* pillars is heavily reinforced and is welded to the floor through wide-flared joints at its base.

Mid-Body Frame

Sport Sedan Pillar Bracing

STRUCTURE

The body sides including the cowl, full-panel doors, rear-quarters, and trunk sides are double-walled for greatest safety and durability. An important feature is their *unitized side-frame construction*. From the cowl to the end of the integral rear fender, each side-frame is precision-built *as a unit* assuring accurate, rattle-free door fits.

The body rear structure is made strong by integral lateral bracing. That of the station wagons is provided by the rigid endgate frame. In the other closed models, the seat-back support, which merges into the parcel shelf, the shelf, which merges into the deck frame, and the frame, which merges into the lower end panel, are all fused together to form a box-like brace between the body sides. Further cross-strength is added by the integral gravel guard, and integral wheelhouses help to form a square-braced rear that is topped by the reinforced trunk lid. The box-sectioned liftgate and double-walled tailgate add strength to the station wagons.

To preserve the strength of every body and to add long years to its life, well-placed

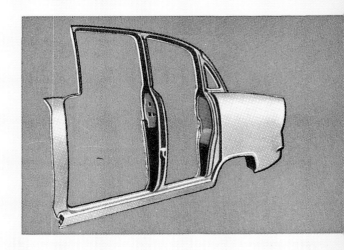

ventilation and drainage holes in all construction pockets prevent water that might seep into the pockets from collecting and rusting through the enclosing metal.

(margin notes) Double-Walled Sides

Rear-Quarter Bracing

Reinforced Lids and Gates

Drainage Holes

LIVE-RUBBER BODY MOUNTINGS

The body is insulated from the jarring effects of rough roads by many live-rubber cushions between the chassis frame and the body structure. These are placed in strategic locations to minimize vibrations without impairing the rigidity of the body-frame combination. The freedom of motion between the body and the frame that is required to obtain

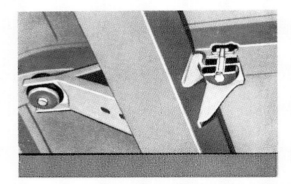

a cushioned ride is slight, so minor frame deflections will cause the body to function as a major reinforcing member of the entire car structure.

Conventional models and sport sedans have 14 rubber cushions. The mounting of the sport sedans differs from that of the conventional models in that the two central body mounts are situated farther to the rear. In their positioning, additional strength is given to the stub-type rear-door hinge pillars by arching the central floor crossbeam rearward to place the mounts under the pillars.

In the sport coupes, to give added rigidity to compensate for the absence of center pillars between the belt line and the steel top, 16 live-rubber cushions are provided.

Because the convertible has no solid steel top, the strength of its extra-rigid Box-Girder chassis frame is utilized to the fullest extent to reinforce the body. This is done by bolting the body solidly to the frame at 20 points at which fiber insulators are provided instead of rubber cushions.

Standard
Body
Mount-
ings

Sport
Coupe
Mountings

Convert-
ible
Mountings

STRUCTURE

BOX-GIRDER CHASSIS FRAME

Frame
Structure

Side-
rails

Cross-
members

Special
Convert-
ible
Frame

Great durability of all car components is promoted by a Box-Girder frame structure that is relatively light in weight but is extraordinarily strong and rigid.

The frame siderails are the double-drop type with the sections between the road wheels at a low level to help provide the extra-low mounting of the body. With a broad box-section that makes them stiff, they extend from bumper to bumper.

The massive front crossmember, also of box section, is both welded and riveted to the siderails. The strengthening arch of the double-walled cowl spans the frame, eliminating need for a crossmember at the rear of the engine. From the cowl to the rear of the body, the body and frame reinforce one another. The heavy rear crossmember, like the front one, is both welded and riveted to the siderails. A special X-structure of I-beams, welded between the siderails, reinforces the frame of the convertible.

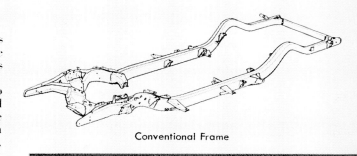

Conventional Frame

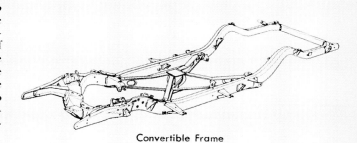

Convertible Frame

MASSIVE WRAPAROUND BUMPERS

Three-
Section
Bumpers

The sturdy, all-steel, channelled bumpers are each made up of three sections, so that, in the event of damage to any *one* section, only that *one* section need be replaced.

Corner
Bracing

Both front and rear bumpers are solidly mounted to the frame ends and are *corner-braced* by rigid diagonal struts that extend outward at an angle from the frame siderails.

Front
Bumper
and
Guards

The front bumper is shaped to the front-end contour. At its sides, where it curves around the fenders, it is deeper to afford more corner protection. The well-spaced bumper guards are bullet-shaped for smart appearance and to help stop bumper locking.

Other
Front-End
Guards

As an accessory, a combined fender and radiator guard spans the car a short distance above the bumper, to give added protection.

Front
Gravel
Guard

To help keep the front of the car clean and to protect it from gravel damage, a shelf-like, horizontal splash-and-gravel guard is formed in the base of the sheet metal to fill the space between the bumper and the body.

Rear
Bumper
and
Guards

The massive rear bumper, with sturdy guards mounted on top, follows the deck contour and wraps around into the car sides. The rear bumper of the station wagons is indented at the center, providing a protective recessed mounting for the license. An accessory guard, like the front fender and radiator guard, adds to rear-end protection.

Rear
Gravel
Guard

Protection from splash and gravel is provided by a ledge that juts from the body to the bumper. Rubber, compressed between the two, makes a water- and dirt-proof seal.

STRUCTURE

STABILIZED FRONT-END STRUCTURE

Front-End Mounting

Supported on a central rubber cushion at its front, the front-end structure rides steady in relation to the body structure, without destructive and annoying weaving. The rigid

Fenders

fenders are solidly bolted to the cowl and connected by a wall of beams to which the radiator is mounted. Their inner walls serve as the sides of the engine compartment. The

Hood

single panel hood is stiffened by flanges at its edges and crossbeams at its ends. By means of counter-balancing, double-acting, gear-type hinges and a safety latch (just to

Hood Operation

the right of center), it may be unlatched and lifted by one hand in an easy continuous motion, and closed and locked in a single movement. The hood opening is both low and broad for easy servicing of the engine.

EXTRA-RIGID CONVERTIBLE CONSTRUCTION

Because the convertible has no rigid top, special steel reinforcements are provided in both its chassis frame and in its body.

The frame is reinforced by the X-structure of I-beams that is welded between the side-rails. The full bracing effect of this X-structure is given to the body by bolting the body solidly to the frame. The rear-quarter of the body itself, is reinforced by side braces from the floor to the door lock pillars and by an extra-rigid reinforcement across the body behind the rear seat. With all these reinforcements, the convertible *without a steel top* weighs 125 pounds more than its companion *hardtop* sport coupe.

The folding top of the convertible is made of a special weather-resistant fabric called *chevrolon*, and is coated with vinyl for beauty, excellent cleanability, and even greater resistance to weather-wear. Stretched taut on its articulating all-steel framework, it is clamped tight to the windshield by a central latch. Rubber at the windshield, and sides that overhang the windows, seal out the weather. The large vinyl-plastic rear window is zipper-fastened at its sides and top so it may be lowered into the well behind the rear seat for breezeway ventilation.

A push-pull knob at the instrument panel activates an electric-hydraulic mechanism that lowers or raises the top. When lowered, the top fits snugly in its well and is covered by a taut snap-on vinyl boot that matches one of the two colors of the upholstery.

To raise the top automatically when the car is unattended and raindrops fall, an electronic device is available as an accessory. The first drops of rain on a moisture-sensitive grid activate the top mechanism. A safety switch prevents unintentional operation.

Convertible Body Structure

Convertible Top

Convertible Top Operation

Convertible Top Raiser

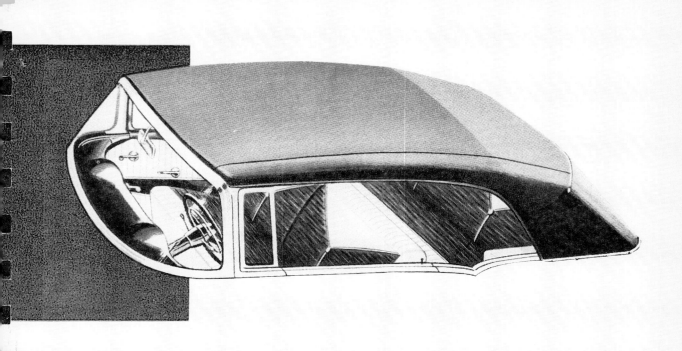

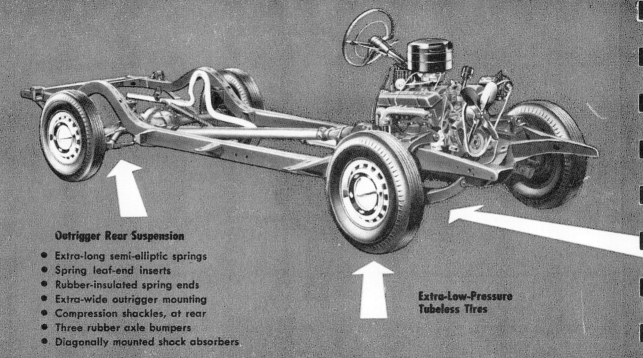

Outrigger Rear Suspension

- Extra-long semi-elliptic springs
- Spring leaf-end inserts
- Rubber-insulated spring ends
- Extra-wide outrigger mounting
- Compression shackles, at rear
- Three rubber axle bumpers
- Diagonally mounted shock absorbers

Extra-Low-Pressure Tubeless Tires

ONLY <u>FOUR</u> LUBRICATION POINTS . . . IN THE <u>WHOLE</u> RIDING SYSTEM

Quadra-Poise Ride

- Seats cradled between wheels
- Broad treads and suspension
- Balanced weight distribution
- Extra-low center of gravity

Glide-Ride Front Suspension

- Inclined Knee-Action coil springs
- Shock absorbers inside springs
- Sealed spherical control-arm outer joints; unique nonmetallic linings
- Rubber-insulated control-arm pivots
- Rubber control-arm bumpers

COMFORTABLE RIDING
. . . on highway or byway!

QUADRA-POISE RIDE

With the seats positioned between the front and rear wheels for the greatest comfort and with balanced weight distribution, the Chevrolet rides smooth and level, cushioned by flexible coil springs at the front and extra-long leaf springs at the rear. The ride is undisturbed by normal road irregularities because the front wheels—each with independent knee action—absorb jarring effects of bumps and holes in the road surface.

Built close to the road, the car has a low center of gravity. This, with extra-wide treads and broad-based rear spring mounting, gives the car unusual stability so it hugs the road on straightaways and curves.

Soft-riding tires, rubber body mountings and flexible seats help to cushion the ride, while the Hotchkiss drive cushions drive-line shocks through the rear springs. Double-acting shock absorbers not only cushion spring action but also stabilize sway and body roll. In addition, rubber mountings absorb engine vibrations, while careful design eliminates transference of vibrations through the driving controls.

Ride Levelizers

Car Stability

Ride Cushioners

SUSPENSION

SOFT-RIDING TUBELESS TIRES

Tire
Construction

Extra-low-pressure tires not only make riding softer, but their tubeless construction makes riding safer because it offers greater resistance to blowouts. Moreover, the tires deflate much more slowly if punctured because an integral butyl rubber liner clings to any sharp object that may penetrate a tire.

Tire Sizes
and Options

The standard tire size is 6.70-15, with a four-ply rating for all models, except for a six-ply rating for the tires of the nine-passenger station wagons. For unusual operating conditions, 6.70-15, 6-ply rating and 7.10-15, 4-ply rating tires are optional. All sizes come with black sidewalls but may be had with optional white outer sidewalls.

Tire
Pressure

The recommended pressure (cold) for the four-ply tires is 24 pounds while that for the six-ply tires is 30 pounds. Uniform pressure in all four tires adds to riding comfort.

Wide-base (five-inch) wheel rims allow straighter tire sidewalls that support the car weight better, provide extra stability to minimize side roll, and increase tire life since *working* of the sidewalls is less severe.

Wheels

Four openings, where the rims join the wheel disks, permit use of strap-on tire chains.

Tire
Tools

Wheel-changing tools include a 1200-pound capacity bumper jack and a combined jack handle and wheel-nut wrench. Both are securely retained so they won't rattle.

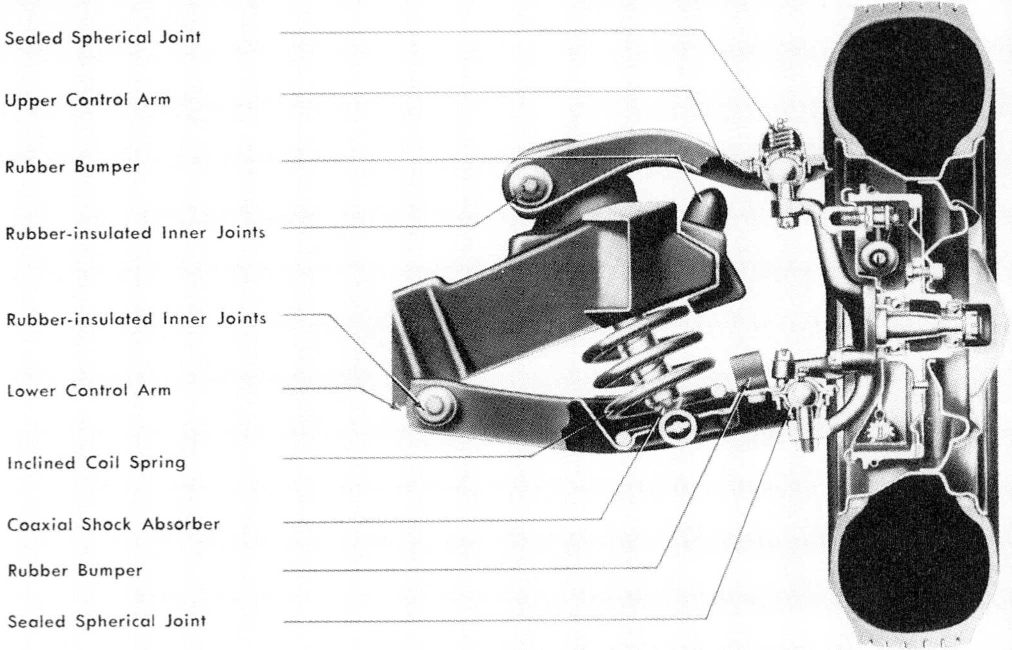

Sealed Spherical Joint

Upper Control Arm

Rubber Bumper

Rubber-insulated Inner Joints

Rubber-insulated Inner Joints

Lower Control Arm

Inclined Coil Spring

Coaxial Shock Absorber

Rubber Bumper

Sealed Spherical Joint

GLIDE-RIDE INDEPENDENT FRONT WHEEL SUSPENSION

Chevrolet's famed Knee-Action allows each front wheel to move up and down independently of the other so it *steps* over any road irregularities in its path. Because of this, the jarring effect of the road irregularities is minimized, the car rides level, and positive control of its direction is maintained.

Coil Springs

Made of tough flexible chrome alloy steel, each coil spring is mounted with its upper end inclined inward. This angular mounting provides greater operating efficiency, increases car stability, and minimizes spring distortion. The upper end of the spring is contained in a *tower* in the chassis frame front crossmember; its lower end is seated in a pocket in the lower control arm.

Spring Control Arms

The spring action is controlled by a short upper control arm and a long lower control arm—both of heavy-gauge pressed steel. At its inner end, each arm hinges on two shock-absorbing rubber-insulated joints; its outer end contains a socket for one of the spherical ends of the forged alloy-steel steering knuckle and wheel spindle on which the road wheel is mounted.

Each spherical joint is a sealed, self-adjusting joint that is lined with a non-metallic bearing material that has exceptionally low friction qualities and resistance to wear. With this type of joint, and this material (molded phenolic-impregnated fabric laminations), the wheels move up and down and turn for steering with ball-bearing ease.

Spherical Joints

Life-lubricated, double-acting hydraulic shock absorbers, mounted inside the coil springs and at the same angle, cushion the spring action and stabilize body sway and roll. They have a large fluid capacity, accurate valve action, and provide excellent ride control in any climate. To absorb the shock of severe jolts, rubber bumpers snub excessive movement of the control arms.

Shock Absorbers

Only four lubrication fitting are required in this suspension, in contrast to the usual 16.

Lube Fittings

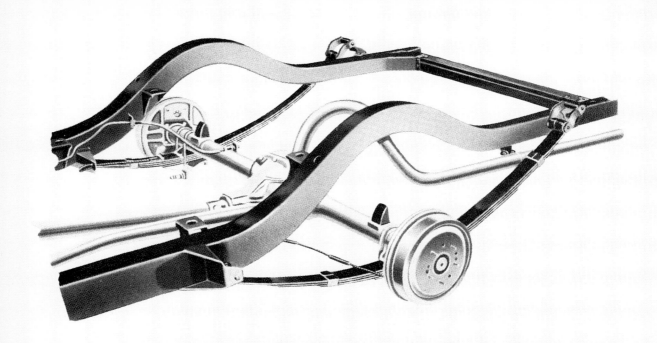

OUTRIGGER REAR SUSPENSION

Spring
Mounting

Sports car stability is provided in the Chevrolet by mounting the parallel, longitudinal rear springs outboard of the chassis frame siderails, instead of in the usual place below them. This locates the springs fully 46 inches apart (center to center) and places them right next to the wide-spaced road wheels. With the springs outside the frame, the frame is lower, helping to lower the body and center of gravity. In addition, the extra-long length of the Chevrolet rear springs contributes to a smoother ride.

Spring
Construction

Of semi-elliptic design, the springs are made up of leaves of tough, resilient chrome alloy steel, with the top leaf shot-peened for greater resistance to flexing fatigue. Spring leaf-end liners, that prevent rubbing of the stacked leaves, and rubber insulation in the mountings of the springs in their front hangers and rear shackles, eliminate any need for lubrication. Compression type shackles provide unhampered spring action.

Shock
Absorbers

Direct-acting shock absorbers, like those in front, control *bottoming* and *pitching*. Diagonally mounted, with their upper ends slanted inward, they provide greater resistance to swaying of the car and have a longer piston travel for better control.

Hotchkiss
Drive

With Hotchkiss drive, the axle and road wheels are connected to the chassis frame *only* through the rear springs. As a result, drive-line shocks are absorbed by the springs.

Spring
Bumpers

To snub severe spring action, three rubber bumpers are mounted above the axle housing: two at its ends, one above its center.

Spring Size
and Leaves

All springs are the same length and width (58″ x 2″) but different numbers of leaves are used in the various models. For sedans and coupes, there are four leaves per spring whereas the greater load capacities of the station wagons require more leaves: five for six-passenger models and six for nine-passenger models. The six-leaf, heavy-duty springs are optional for the other models.

THREE GREAT VALVE-IN-HEAD ENGINES

"Turbo-Fire V8"

"Super Turbo-Fire V8"

"Blue-Flame 140"

SUPERIOR PERFORMANCE . . . GAS-SAVING ECONOMY . . . LONG-LASTING DEPENDABILITY

- High-compression power
- High power-to-weight ratio
- Positive-Shift starting
- Super-efficient breathing

- 12-Volt all-weather ignition
- High-Turbulence combustion
- Fast, quiet exhaust discharge
- Rigid powerplant structure

- Smoothly moving parts
- Controlled pressure lubrication
- Power-Hushed cooling
- Poised-Power engine mounts

NOTE: A complete composite feature list is provided at the end of this section.

AMERICA'S
MOST MODERN ENGINES
. . . for thrilling driving pleasure!

3 POWERFUL ENGINES

Engine Selection

For 1956, Chevrolet offers a wide choice of power (*see Size section*) in three great engines. Where the preference is for an overhead valve V8, the choice is between two of the industry's finest powerplants—the action-packed "Turbo-Fire V8" or the hotter-than-ever "Super Turbo-Fire V8." For those who prefer a six, Chevrolet presents the high-stepping "Blue-Flame 140"—one of the most advanced valve-in-head sixes ever designed.

Valve-in-head Leadership

Each of these engines is alive with high-compression power . . . for brilliant acceleration, swift safe passing, and effortless cruising on hill or highway. Each combines outstanding performance with welcome fuel economy and traditional Chevrolet durability. These three great engines in every detail reflect the 42 years of valve-in-head engine design leadership by Chevrolet—builder of more valve-in-head engines than all other manufacturers combined.

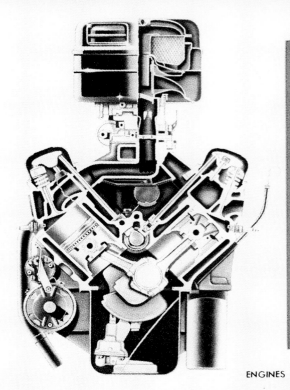

ACTION-PACKED "TURBO-FIRE V8"

The high-compression power of the advanced "Turbo-Fire V8" provides brilliant performance that sets the pace in every price class.

Cylinder Block

Scientific engineering has achieved space-saving compactness and low engine weight in the design of the V8 cylinder block. Cast of alloy iron, the short, rigid block features an extra-large bore of 3.75 inches. Combined with the short piston stroke of 3.0 inches—shortest of any passenger car in the industry—the efficient 265-cubic-inch displacement contributes to the husky torque output and flashing performance of this outstanding engine. Short-stroke design means less friction, less heat loss, and less vibration—and makes the delivery of power smoother.

Cylinder Heads

The cylinder heads, of cast alloy iron, have high-turbulence Fire-Swirl combustion chambers of a wedge-shape that assures fast, complete burning of the fuel mixture. Water passages provide full-circuit cooling between the heads and cylinder block.

Compression Ratio

The high (8.0 to 1) compression ratio extracts more power from less fuel.

Crankshaft

The extra-rigid, forged steel crankshaft, including its counterweights, is carefully machined to precision tolerances. Five main bearings provide accurate crankshaft alignment. A vibration damper, called the *Harmonic Balancer*, absorbs power impulses to assure smooth engine operation.

Connecting Rods

The extremely short distance from the crankshaft center to the bottom of the cylinder bores permits the use of short, light, rigid connecting rods. Pressed-in, chromium-steel piston pins permit greater connecting rod strength and durability.

Pistons

The slipper-skirt aluminum-alloy pistons have been developed for extreme lightness, rapid heat dissipation and exceptional bearing durability. Integral steel struts control their expansion in the cylinder bores. The piston pins are offset from the piston centers to prevent noisy, injurious piston slap.

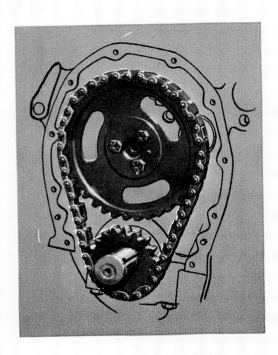

The two compression rings of each piston are taper faced, and the top ring is flash-chromed to minimize cylinder wall scuffing during the engine break-in period. The oil control ring is fully chrome-plated for extra life, and is designed to provide maximum oil control, to exclude engine oil from the combustion chambers under all conditions.

Piston
Rings

The durable cast alloy iron camshaft revolves on five bearings and is maintained in split-second synchronization with the crankshaft through a silent chain drive. This results in precise timing and accurate valve operation. With Powerglide, a new, higher lift camshaft permits more fuel mixture to enter the combustion chambers to provide more power for high-speed operation.

Camshaft
and
Timing
Chain

Chevrolet's V8 valve train mechanism is advanced far beyond its price class. Exclusive to Chevrolet in the low-price field, every valve has its own completely independent operating mechanism. This includes the hydraulic valve lifter, low-weight push rod, individually mounted rocker arm of pressed steel, and variable-pitch valve spring.

Valve
Mechanism

ENGINES (V8)

Exhaust Valves

The exhaust valves are made of extra-alloy steel, for greater heat resistance and durability. In addition, they are aluminum-dipped—an exclusive Chevrolet process in the low-price field—so they resist pitting and combustion deposits.

Valve Lifters

Hydraulic-Hushed valve lifters that eliminate annoying tappet sounds are standard with every Chevrolet engine for 1956. With them, zero valve clearance is automatically maintained, making periodic tappet adjustments no longer a requirement.

Engine Bearings

The engine bearings are the precision-replaceable, steel-backed babbitt insert type. Not only are they extra-durable, but they are easy to replace, if necessary.

Engine Lubrication

Scientific lubrication contributes greatly to the engine's outstanding efficiency and durability. The controlled full-pressure lubrication system requires only four quarts of oil for refill. With it, each moving part is supplied the correct amount of oil at precisely the right

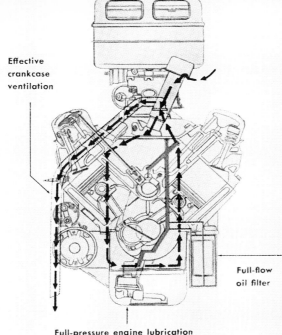

Effective
crankcase
ventilation

Full-flow
oil filter

Full-pressure engine lubrication

time, and under the most effective pressure. The main oil gallery is supplied directly from the screened gear-type oil pump and distributes a pressurized flow of oil throughout the engine. Hydraulic valve lifter oil galleries receive a constant supply of pressurized oil for lubrication of rocker arms and valves. Pressure lubrication of connecting rod bearings and cylinder walls is effected through drilled passages in the crankshaft. A welded-in oil pan baffle prevents oil surging on quick braking and reduces oil-foaming.

With the new full-flow oil filter, an option that is now available on all V8's, all oil is completely filtered before reaching the lubrication points, extending the life of every moving part. The easily replaceable filter element permits rapid oil passage.

Oil Filter

Effective crankcase ventilation removes harmful vapors through an external road draft tube. Vapor removal is thorough and the engine oil is kept fresh longer.

Crankcase Ventilation

ENGINES (V8)

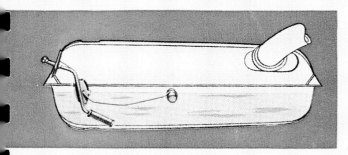

of indrawn air for extra-quiet operation.

The engine features a two-barrel, down-draft carburetor with an improved automatic choke. Dual carburetion contributes to Chevrolet's outstanding V8 performance by assuring balanced fuel flow at all driving speeds. A special exhaust cross-over in the intake manifold conveys heat for prevention of icing during warmup. The intake manifold design insures uniform fuel mixture distribution to each cylinder.

Carburetor

The engine is started by a turn of the ignition key. The all-weather ignition system insures quick, dependable, year-around starting and a reliable spark at all speeds. Featured are a 12-volt battery, the high-speed Positive-Shift starter, a high-capacity generator, and spark plugs with large, durable electrodes. For 1956, the system is improved by new battery and spark plug designs and by waterproofing the starter solenoid and voltage regulator in addition to the other parts of the system. In all, no finer ignition system exists on any car—in any price class!

Ignition System

Gas Tank

A large-area filter screen, incorporated in the gasoline tank rather than in the fuel pump, protects the entire fuel system from foreign matter as well as water that could freeze in the gas lines. The gasoline tank capacity is 16 gallons (17 in station wagons).

Fuel Pump and Air Cleaner

The pulsator-type fuel pump provides a smooth, constant flow of fuel to the carburetor, while an efficient oil-bath air cleaner filters and silences the flow of air into the carburetor. For 1956, an external shroud added to the air cleaner reduces the sound

ENGINES (V8)

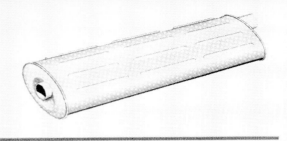

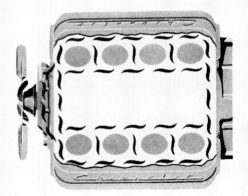

The reverse-flow Power-Tone muffler minimizes power-robbing back pressure. Extra long—30 inches (24 inches in the convertible) —and with triple resonance chambers, it effectively hushes exhaust sounds. The entire exhaust system is flexibly suspended on rubber-insulated mountings that absorb vibrations, making the system more durable.

Exhaust System

Because Chevrolet valve-in-head engines are so highly efficient, more combustion force is converted into usable power—leaving less heat to be absorbed by the cooling system. In any climate, the engine quickly attains the proper operating temperature. And through controlled air and coolant circulation, this temperature is maintained —assuring maximum power, economy, and engine durability. Outstanding cooling features include a low, wide, free-flow radiator with 16-quart coolant capacity (17 with

Cooling System

heater); a high-capacity by-pass type water pump for maintenance of proper coolant circulation at lower speeds; full-length water jackets surrounding all cylinders; water passages encircling all valve seats, assuring constant cooling of these critical points; a large diameter fan that revolves more slowly to keep fan roar at a minimum; and a pressure-type radiator cap that increases cooling capacity under extreme conditions. A new electrical gauge on the instrument panel provides more accurate temperature indication at all times.

Engine
Balancing

Exceptional dynamic balance is built into every "Turbo-Fire V8." During assembly, the engine's individual parts are carefully weight-matched and balanced to exacting standards. Then, each assembled engine is placed in motion and electronically balanced by a giant machine developed especially for this operation. The final result is a smoother, quieter, and finer-performing engine.

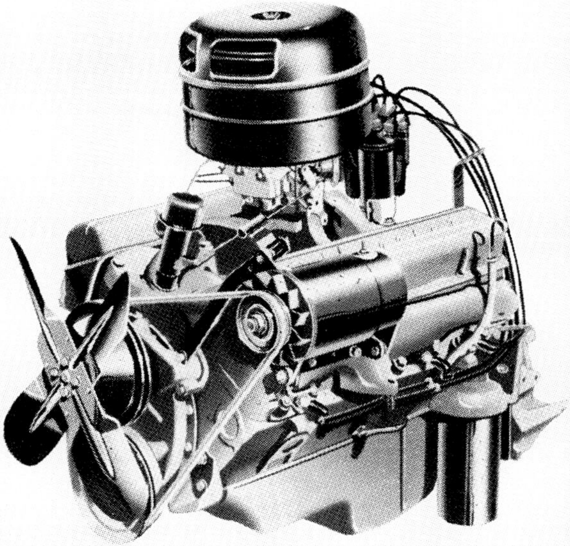

ENGINES (V8)

HOTTER THAN EVER!

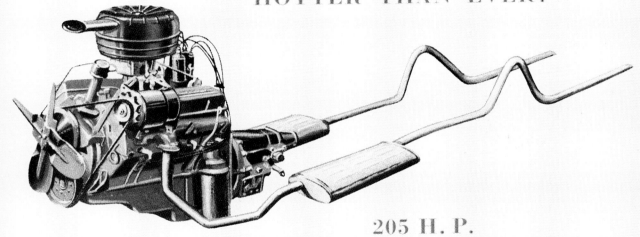

205 H. P.
"SUPER TURBO-FIRE V8"

ENGINES (V8)

For those who want exceptional performance, the "Super Turbo-Fire V8" (Option 410) is it! In traffic, on the toughest hills, or on long straightaways, this engine takes over with a surging *go* of masterful performance. All the advanced basic Chevrolet V8 design features are here—PLUS:

Cylinder Head

A *special* cylinder head gives the engine an ultra-high compression ratio of 9.25 to 1.

Camshaft

A *special* higher lift camshaft permits deeper engine breathing, which results in the greatly increased power output.

Carbu-retor

A *special* four-barrel downdraft carburetor supplies proper mixture volume in high speed operation and under extreme acceleration. Basically two dual carburetors combined with an automatic choke in one assembly, this high-performance carburetor provides two supplementary barrels which come into operation when the accelerator pedal is fully depressed for top performance.

Intake Manifold

A *special* intake manifold provides 15 percent larger fuel intake passages, permitting denser intake mixtures with high velocity at high engine speeds. This assures each cylinder its full charge of fuel-air mixture at even the highest engine speeds.

Air Cleaner

A *special* heavy-duty oil-bath air cleaner assures that dust and dirt are screened from the carburetion system, providing maximum engine protection at all times.

Exhaust System

A *special* dual exhaust system completes the increased breathing efficiency of the engine. Twin exhaust pipes are welded individually to each of the two reverse-flow Power-Tone mufflers. Effective quieting of the exhaust is achieved through the use of triple hush chambers in each muffler. To avoid drawing of fumes into the body when station wagons are driven with the endgates open, the dual exhaust tailpipes of these models are designed to discharge the fumes into the slipstreams of the rear wheels.

HIGH-STEPPING
"BLUE-FLAME 140"

The culmination of 42 years of industry-pacing design and superior manufacture, the great new Chevrolet "Blue-Flame 140" valve-in-head engine, with its new higher compression ratio of 8.0 to 1, brings to the six-cylinder field brilliant new concepts of performance, economy and durability.

Relatively simple in design, it is the proved *in-line* type, built around an extremely rigid cast alloy iron cylinder block, in which full-length water jackets around each cylinder barrel provide for maximum uniform cooling of all pistons. The cylinder bore of 3.56 inches and piston stroke of 3.94 inches give a total displacement of 235.5 cubic inches.

Cylinder Block

Scientifically designed combustion chambers, of a modified wedge shape, permit higher conversion of fuel mixture explosions into power, and are an important reason for Chevrolet's famous fuel economy.

Combustion Chambers

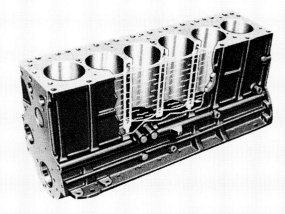

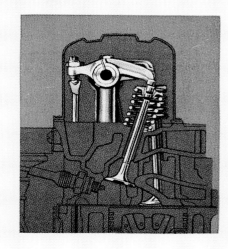

Cylinder Head

Proved Chevrolet valve-in-head design permits the use of large valves for high volumetric efficiency, permitting a generous flow of gases to and from the combustion chambers with every intake and exhaust stroke.

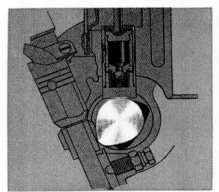

The backbone of the engine is the carefully balanced, rugged drop-forged steel crankshaft with four main bearings. Its great stiffness assures smooth performance even at high engine speeds. A crankshaft-mounted vibration damper damps impulses to keep the flow of power smooth and quiet.

Crankshaft

A new higher lift, cast alloy iron camshaft allows deeper-breathing and greater power output. Silent-mesh helical gears—composition on camshaft, steel on crankshaft—assure a synchronized camshaft drive. Valve timing is precise at all speeds.

Camshaft

168

Valve Mechanism

With hydraulic valve lifters, tappet sounds are automatically minimized by the zero clearance, and the need for periodic adjustments is eliminated. Short, one-piece push rods, precision-bored rocker arms, and variable-pitch valve springs add effectively to improved valve train operation and overall powerplant performance.

Valves

For maximum precision at high engine temperatures, the exhaust valves are made of special extra-alloy steel. To protect against combustion deposits and pitting, they are aluminum-dipped—an exclusive Chevrolet process in the low-price field—which definitely increases valve life.

Pistons

The full-skirt aluminum pistons have been developed for rapid heat dissipation and reduced bearing loads. Offset piston pins assure quiet operation. Piston surfaces are tin-coated for wear resistance. Integral steel struts control the expansion of the pistons, maintaining their precise fit in the cylinders.

ENGINES (6)

The three piston rings include two compression rings formed of thick-wall cast alloy iron and a steel rail-type oil control ring, chrome plated for extra durability. A spring-steel expander gives maximum oil control under all driving conditions.

Drop-forged steel connecting rods with precision insert bearings add strength and durability. A special locking device secures the chrome steel piston pins to the rods.

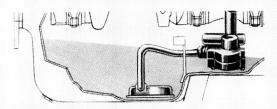

The full-pressure lubrication system armors the engine parts in oil at all speeds. A camshaft-driven gear pump with fixed screen intake picks up clean oil and forces it under controlled pressure into the main oil gallery. The pressurized oil then flows through each main bearing to the camshaft bearings, and to the connecting rods and cylinder walls through drilled passages. Oil from the camshaft rear bearing supplies the valve-lifter gallery and is metered to the overhead valve system. Positive lubrication of the timing gears is effected by a pressurized oil spray jet. A welded-in oil pan baffle is designed to prevent surging and foaming of oil. A replaceable-element oil filter (Option 237) is available to help keep the oil clean.

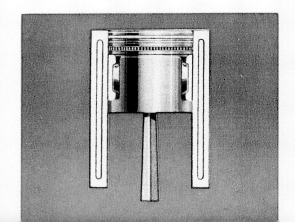

Crankcase ventilating air enters through an oil filler cap, with a filtered intake, on top of the engine. Air flowing through the crankcase picks up harmful vapors which are carried away by the vehicle air stream.

The gasoline tank capacity is a generous 16 gallons (17 in station wagons), and the fuel system is protected from foreign matter and water by a special filter in the tank. The pulsator-type fuel pump delivers a smooth constant flow of gasoline to the carburetor.

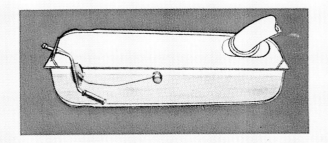

An oil-wetted air cleaner filters and silences the air flow into the carburetor. An oil-bath air cleaner (Option 216) provides for operation in dust-laden air. The automatic choke makes starting and warmups quick and convenient in all weather. Twin concentric carburetor floats maintain a balanced fuel mixture even on curves and grades.

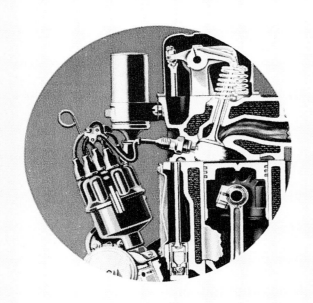

The intake manifold is designed to provide balanced fuel-mixture distribution. Stellar performance is attained through full-charge combustion in every cylinder at all engine speeds.

Intake Manifold

Chevrolet's powerful, modern 12-volt electrical system doubly insures easy year-round starting, and dependable high-speed ignition. The efficient high-capacity generator, husky 12-volt battery, High-Tower distributor, weather-sealed coil, automatic spark control, and special wiring, deliver an extra-powerful, precisely timed spark for reliable ignition at even the highest speeds. For 1956, a longer-life battery and waterproofing of the starter and the voltage regulator provide even more dependable ignition.

Ignition System

The exhaust system is scientifically designed to provide rapid, thorough, quiet exhaust. Low-resistance passages in the exhaust manifold and a unitized exhaust pipe

Exhaust System

ENGINES (6)

conduct the gases to the muffler where reverse-flow action minimizes back-pressure. Exhaust noise is hushed by three resonance chambers in the muffler. Flexible mounts absorb vibrations, making the system more durable.

The engine features integral by-pass cooling with a high-capacity pump for accurate temperature control, large-volume low speed circulation, and smooth, quick engine warm-up. The large-diameter fan is designed for high-volume air flow at low fan speeds. Its quiet operation and low power consumption add to the engine's smooth performance.

A highly accurate electrical temperature indicator, on the instrument panel, functions when the ignition switch is turned on.

POISED-POWER MOUNTINGS FOR ALL ENGINES

Chevrolet's Poised-Power engine mountings cushion powerplant movements and isolate the chassis frame and car body from annoying vibrations. The scientifically designed four-point suspension system poises the entire engine on large rubber mountings located at strategic balance points. For 1956, improved rear mountings provide even greater insulation from sounds and vibration, and include a rebound feature that provides better control of engine movement.

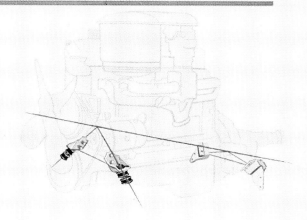

STAR FEATURES OF

Feature	"Blue Flame 140"	"Turbo-Fire V8"	"Super Turbo-Fire V8"
MOST MODERN ENGINE DESIGN			
Six-in-line, valve-in-head engine.	★		
90° V8 valve-in-head engine.		★	★
Exceptionally short stroke.	★	★ ★	★ ★
High power-to-weight ratio.	★ ★	★ ★	★ ★
8 to 1 compression ratio.	★		
9.25 to 1 compression ratio.		★	★
Compact, rigid engine structure.	★	★	★
Engine balanced as an assembly.		★	★ ★
Four-point rubber engine mounting.	★	★ ★	★ ★
SMOOTH-TURNING ROTATING PARTS			
Precision-balanced rotating parts.		★	★
Four-bearing, forged steel crankshaft.	★		
Five-bearing, forged steel crankshaft.		★ ★ ★	★ ★ ★
Precision-interchangeable bearings.		★	★
Oscillating crankshaft vibration damper.			★
Cast alloy iron camshaft.	★	★ ★ ★	★ ★ ★ ★
Silent helical timing gears.	★		
Silent timing chain.		★	★
LIGHTWEIGHT RECIPROCATING PARTS			
Matched piston and connecting rod sets.	★	★ ★	★ ★ ★
Tin-plated aluminum pistons with full skirts.		★	★
Tin-plated aluminum pistons with slipper skirts.			★
Three super-sealing rings per piston.	★	★	★
Locked-in-rod, offset, chrome steel piston pins.		★	★
Pressed-in-rod, offset, chrome steel piston pins.	★		
Rigid forged steel connecting rods.	★	★ ★	★ ★
Precision-interchangeable rod bearings.		★	★
SUPER-SILENT VALVE TRAINS			
Valve trains with rocker arms operating on single shaft.	★		
Separate, individual valve trains.		★	★
Hardened valve train contact surfaces.		★	★
Hydraulic valve lifters.	★	★ ★	★ ★ ★
Short, one-piece, upset-ended push rods.	★		
Short, tubular push rods carrying oil to valves.		★	★
Precision-bored Ar-Ma-Steel rocker arms.		★ ★	★ ★
Unique pressed steel rocker arms.	★		
Aluminum-dipped, extra-alloy exhaust valves.		★ ★ ★	★ ★ ★ ★
Silchrome or nickel-chrome intake valves.	★	★ ★	★ ★ ★
Removable steel valve guides.	★		
Valve guides integral with head.		★	★
Variable-pitch valve springs.	★ ★	★ ★	★ ★
Coined-steel spring caps with split-collar locks.		★	★
Rubber valve stem seals.		★	★
CONTROLLED LUBRICATION			
Full-pressure lubrication.	★ ★ ★	★ ★ ★	★ ★ ★
Red oil-pressure warning light.		★ ★	★ ★
Top-of-engine oil filler with crankcase breather.	★		
Five-quart refill capacity.		★	★
Four-quart refill capacity.	★		
Handy bayonet oil level gauge rod.		★ ★ ★	★ ★ ★
Camshaft-driven gear oil pump with screened intake.	★ ★	★ ★	★ ★
By-pass type oil filter (option).		★	★
Full-flow oil filter (option).		★	★
Roaddraft crankcase ventilation.	★	★ ★	★ ★

EFFICIENT GASOLINE SUPPLY SYSTEM

- 16-gallon tank with filter; 17, station wagons
- Left-hand taillight gas filler
- Cam-action filler cap; accessory lockable cap
- Accurate electric gas gauge
- Adjustment to suit octane rating of gasoline
- Pulsator-type camshaft-driven fuel pump

SUPERIOR CARBURETION

- Oil-wetted air cleaner with silencer; optional oil-bath air cleaner
- Oil-bath air cleaner with silencer and shroud
- Concentric-bowl downdraft carburetor
- Dual downdraft carburetor
- High-performance four-barrel downdraft carburetor
- Automatic choke
- Carburetor fast-idle mechanism
- Carburetor warmup de-icing
- Automatic fuel mixture heat control
- Three-port, level-with-ground intake manifold
- Double-deck manifold with equalized passages
- Special double-deck manifold; equalized passages

HIGH-VOLTAGE SURE-FIRE IGNITION

- 12-Volt all-weather ignition
- High-speed Positive-Shift starter
- Dual automatic spark control
- Heavy-duty spark plugs
- High-turbulence, wedge-shaped combustion chambers

QUICK-DISCHARGE EXHAUST SYSTEM

- Low-resistance passages in exhaust manifold
- Single exhaust system
- Single exhaust system with cross-under pipe
- Dual exhaust system
- Integral exhaust pipe and muffler
- Resonance-type reverse-flow muffler
- Full-length tailpipe
- Flexible exhaust system suspension

POWER-HUSHED COOLING

- Free-flow, ribbed-cellular radiator
- Pressure radiator cap
- Quiet, staggered four-blade fan
- Slower-than-engine fan speed
- Narrow V-section fan belt
- Vibration-free bellows thermostat
- Bypass cooling recirculation
- Life-lubricated ball-bearing water pump
- Dual water pump discharge passages into block
- Full-depth water jackets around all cylinders
- Valve seats entirely surrounded with water
- Accurate electric temperature gauge

EASY ENGINE SERVICING

- Counterbalanced hood; external release, positive lock
- Large working area in engine compartment
- Automatic underhood light accessory

THREE-STAR PERFORMERS

NINE POWER TEAMS	1	2	3	4	5	6	7	8	9
OPTIONS*	Standard	221	221 and 410	315	222 and 315	222, 315, 410	313	223 and 313	223, 313, 410
ENGINE	140-hp "Blue-Flame" 6	162-hp "Turbo-Fire V8"	205-hp "Super Turbo-Fire V8"	140-hp "Blue-Flame" 6	162-hp "Turbo-Fire V8"	205-hp "Super Turbo-Fire V8"	140-hp "Blue-Flame" 6	170-hp "Turbo-Fire V8"	205-hp "Super Turbo-Fire V8"
CLUTCH	9½" diameter	10" diameter		9½" diameter	10" diameter		None		
CLUTCH	Tip-Toe-Matic clutch with easy diaphragm spring actuation. Heavy-duty coil spring (clutch) on "Super Turbo-Fire V8". Life-lubricated ball release bearing. Suspended pedal.						None		
TRANS-MISSION	Quiet-Ease Synchro-Mesh transmission: Three speeds. Extra-quiet, hardened and shot-peened helical gears in all speeds. Synchro-Mesh second and third speed gears. Steering-column gearshift lever.			Touch-Down Overdrive transmission: Three-speed Synchro-Mesh transmission with three-pinion planetary-gear overdrive providing semi-automatic fourth speed. Steering-column gearshift lever. Direct-pull lockout handle. Electric engagement, controlled by accelerator.			Super-Smooth Powerglide automatic transmission: Hydraulic, three-element torque converter. Helical planetary gears for reverse and low. Controlled oil cooling. Positive parking lock. Starter safety switch. Steering-column selector lever. Lighted, P-N-D-L-R selector dial in instrument cluster.		
DRIVE	Hotchkiss drive: Tubular propeller shaft. Two needle-bearing universal joints.								
AXLE	Fuel-Saver axle (3.7 to 1 ratio)			Power-Master axle (4.11 to 1 ratio)			Economizer axle (3.55 to 1 ratio)		
AXLE	Quiet, durable hypoid drive gears Two-pinion differential. Extra-strong axle shafts with integral, flanged wheel hubs. Semi-floating axle ends. Single-unit banjo housing. Six anti-friction bearings.								

*221, 222, or 223—V8 engine with indicated transmission; 313—Powerglide; 315—Overdrive; 410—V8 power package.

RELATIVE POWER TEAM ADVANTAGES

1. Fine, economical performance, with easy, manual gearshifting.
2. Remarkable performance at lowest cost, with easy, manual gearshifting.
3. The maximum in thrilling, low-cost power, with easy, manual gearshifting.
4. Wonderful performance, with big gas savings and small upkeep, plus simplified gearshifting.
5. Marvelous performance, operating and upkeep economy, and simplified gearshifting.
6. Superb performance with extraordinary overall economy, and simplified gearshifting.
7. Fine, economical performance, with automatic driving at lowest cost.
8. An excellent combination of high-compression power, economy, and automatic driving.
9. All the convenience of automatic driving at its best . . . with brilliant acceleration, effortless cruising, and outstanding economy of operation.

A choice of
NINE DIFFERENT
POWER TEAMS
. . . for every kind of driving!

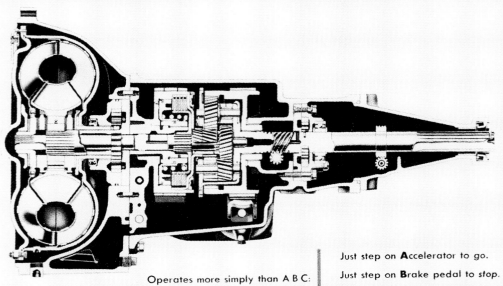

Operates more simply than A B C:

Just step on **A**ccelerator to go.

Just step on **B**rake pedal to stop.

There is no **C**lutch pedal to operate.

SUPER-SMOOTH
POWERGLIDE AUTOMATIC TRANSMISSION

Brilliant acceleration; quiet, effortless cruising; and remarkable operating economy make Chevrolet's Powerglide (Option 313) outstanding among automatic transmissions. The Chevrolet Powerglide ride is a proved ride—billions of miles of proof experienced by more than two million owners who have made it their automatic choice—and the most enjoyable way of motoring today.

Still the simplest automatic transmission in the low-price field, Powerglide's superior design centers on three basic units, which are combined to give no-shift driving at its simplest and most convenient best:

Torque Converter

(1) The high-efficiency torque converter automatically transmits engine power to the axle, with a smooth transition from standstill to full speed—completely free of any direct mechanical connection to the engine.

Planetary Gears

(2) The planetary gearset operates automatically when getaway power or greater acceleration for safe, swift passing is needed. In *low*, it almost doubles engine torque and, in *reverse*, it permits fully controlled backing.

Hydraulic Control System

(3) In *drive*, the hydraulic control system automatically selects the proper range—either low or cruising—to suit the driving conditions. The *low* band and *drive* range clutch are actuated according to the car speed and accelerator pedal pressure. Engine power is matched to the driving needs, automatically, smoothly, and efficiently.

Other Features

Other Powerglide features are the positive parking lock; starting in either *park* or *neutral*; and, for ease in getting out of sand or snow, the convenient arrangements of *low* and *reverse* in adjacent selector positions.

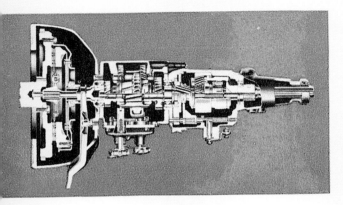

TOUCH-DOWN
OVERDRIVE TRANSMISSION

Overdrive Unit

Chevrolet's overdrive transmission (Option 315) is essentially a three-speed Synchro-Mesh transmission combined with a planetary gear overdrive unit that provides a semi-automatic fourth speed. In *overdrive*, with a ratio of 0.7 to 1, engine speed is reduced more than 22 percent less than with the standard Synchro-Mesh transmission. Thus, gasoline mileage is increased, and engine wear and oil consumption are reduced.

Overdrive Ratio

With the convenient T-handle overdrive control pushed in, a momentary release of accelerator pedal pressure above 30 miles per hour automatically engages the overdrive with consequent smoothness and quieter engine operation at all cruising speeds. Touch-down acceleration is afforded by fully depressing the accelerator pedal, thus automatically downshifting into direct drive for extra-swift passing, hill climbing or emergency power. A momentary release of the accelerator quickly and smoothly re-engages the overdrive. For simplified shifting in traffic, at speeds below 30 miles per hour, the clutch pedal need be depressed only when starting from a standstill or for full stops. Shifting is simply a matter of releasing the accelerator pedal, moving the shift lever, and depressing the accelerator pedal again.

Overdrive Operation

POWER TEAMS

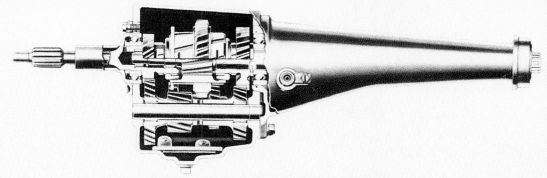

QUIET-EASE SYNCHRO-MESH TRANSMISSION

Chevrolet's famous three-speed Synchro-Mesh transmission teams up with any of the three great engines to provide thrifty, smooth performance at the lowest cost of all power teams. Embracing the constant-mesh principle, this heavy-duty transmission is engineered so that the moving parts are perfectly synchronized—brought to the same speed of rotation—before gear engagement. Major design features include a large diam-eter output shaft, large rear support bearing for high load-carrying capacity, and special mounting for extra rigidity of the complete engine-clutch-transmission assembly. All gears are shot-peened after hardening. Gear teeth ends are rounded to provide smooth, quiet meshing with less friction. And a particle-trapping baffle at the bottom of the transmission case guards against damage to gear teeth and bearings.

Synchroni-zation

Features

Gears

SMOOTH-OPERATING CLUTCHES

DIAPHRAGM SPRING CLUTCH

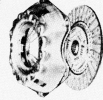

COIL SPRING CLUTCH

The "Turbo-Fire V8" and "Blue-Flame 140" engines, with either Synchro-Mesh or Overdrive, feature the famous Chevrolet diaphragm spring clutch, proved by millions of miles of smooth, shock-free power-transmission. The "Turbo-Fire V8" clutch disk is 10 inches in diameter and has a new woven asbestos facing for smooth engagement and efficient power transfer at higher engine speeds and greater torque conditions. A large 9½-inch molded asbestos clutch disk facing is used with the "Blue-Flame 140." An 11-inch diaphragm spring clutch (Option 227) is obtainable with either engine for heavy-duty operations. Clutch operation is smooth and easy, requiring little pedal pressure.

To match the higher power of the "Super Turbo-Fire V8," a new extra-heavy-duty coil-spring clutch provides greater capacity through nine heat-treated coil springs and a larger area, 11-inch diameter disk. Engineered pressure plate surface ventilation is an added feature of this high-capacity clutch.

All clutches feature a more rigid, thicker steel clutch fork for greater durability and more positive operation. Advanced clutch linkage design minimizes annoying transfer of engine vibrations through the pedal, adding to Chevrolet's notable driving comfort.

EFFICIENT
HOTCHKISS DRIVE

Engine torque is transmitted to the axle through the tubular propeller shaft and two needle-bearing universal joints of the Hotchkiss drive system. In addition to contributing to low car height, Hotchkiss drive cushions torque transfer and smoothes the ride.

QUIET HYPOID AXLE

All models feature a semi-floating axle, with hypoid drive gears, a two-pinion differential, flanged axle shafts, and a unitized banjo housing. The gear ratios are engineered to each power team: 3.70 to 1 with Synchro-Mesh; 4.11 to 1 with Overdrive; and 3.55 to 1 with Powerglide. The welded-on axle housing cover combines high structural rigidity with complete elimination of oil leakage. Specially designed wheel bearing oil seals make the axle practically leakproof.

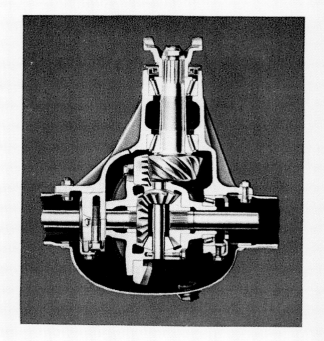

PRECISION CAR CONTROL

Extra-Easy
Ball-Race Steering

- Street-width turning circle
- Large overall steering ratio
- Spherical joints with nonmetallic linings
- Equal-length steering tie-rods
- Easy-turning, recirculating ball-nut steering gear
- Man-size, deep-hub steering wheel; handy horn controls
- Optional Power-Touch hydraulic-power steering

. . . for GREATER DRIVING SAFETY!

**Velvet-Pressure
Jumbo-Drum Brakes**

- Eleven-inch brakes at all wheels
- Cast iron and steel drums
- Self-energizing brake shoes
- Long-lasting bonded linings
- Perfected hydraulic actuation
- Dash-mounted master cylinder
- Suspended brake pedal
- Anti-Dive braking control
- Optional Pivot-Pedal vacuum-power braking
- Direct-acting parking brakes
- Parking brake pull-handle
- Accessory parking brake signal

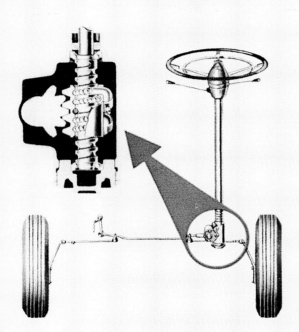

BALL-RACE STEERING

The 1956 Chevrolet steers smoothly, with remarkable ease, and returns to *straight ahead* once a turn is made. The turning diameter is small: 41½ feet (curb to curb), 44½ feet (wall to wall). The large overall steering ratio (25.7 to 1) helps to make steering easy. And the lightweight Chevrolet engines impose no extra turning burden on the front wheels. But the major contributor to the wonderful steerability of the car is its steering mechanism—highly efficient from road wheels to steering wheel.

At the road wheels, the sealed, self-adjusting, spherical joints of the front suspension unit serve in place of ordinary steering knuckles. Their Chevrolet-pioneered, nonmetallic linings have excellent anti-friction and durability qualities that assure continued easy turning of the wheels. In *every* model, the rigid relay-type linkage, which connects the wheels, has equal-length tie

Turning
Circle

Overall
Steering
Ratio

Spherical
Joints

Steering
Linkage

CONTROLS

rods for better steering balance under all driving conditions. Self-adjusting spherical bearings throughout the linkage add to steering ease. A feature usually found only in high-priced cars is the Ball-Race steering gear (ratio, 20 to 1) in which ball bearings reduce friction to a minimum to make steering smoother and much easier.

All steering wheels are the deep-hub type, with the hubs recessed for safety, better appearance, and a better view of the instruments. Of hard rubber on a steel frame, they are a foot-and-a-half in diameter, with three spokes in Bel Air models and two in the "Two-Ten" and "One-Fifty" series. Deep finger notches in their rims assure a firm, comfortable grip. The full-circle horn-blowing ring of Bel Air and "Two-Ten" models, and the large horn button of the "One-Fifty" models assure quick horn-sounding regardless of the wheel position. For greater safety, too, *two* matched horns are provided in *all* models. In addition, a third horn is available as an accessory. It is a 12-inch trumpet-type

vibrator horn with a frequency that blends with those of the standard horns to produce a pleasing tone that warns but does not startle. For neatness, the steering column for *every* Chevrolet encloses the mechanism for the transmission and turn-signal controls.

POWER-TOUCH STEERING

Steering is even easier with Chevrolet's hydraulic power steering (Option 324), in which the power cylinder is built right into the standard steering linkage. This linkage-type design provides all the driver advantages, yet is simpler than the complicated integral types used in some other cars. Moreover, being located outside the engine compartment, it is easier to service and doesn't hamper work on the engine.

Whenever more than *three* pounds of effort is required, the power begins to function and provides up to 80 percent assistance in steer-

Steering Gear

Steering Wheel

Horns

Steering Column

Linkage-Type Power Steering

Steering Effort

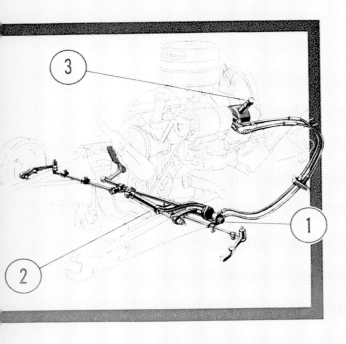

ing the car. The unit acts directly on the steering linkage, and all its components are located in the part of the linkage where they are most effective. The hydraulic control valve (1) and the hydraulic-power cylinder (2) are connected directly to the steering relay link. Hence, road shocks, rather than being transmitted into the steering column, are cushioned by the cylinder before reaching the driver's hands. The vane-type pressure supply pump (3), which is driven by a heavy-duty generator, produces hydraulic pressure of over 750 pounds whenever required—for effortless parking and driving that's more relaxing, more enjoyable. Either the 30-ampere generator (Option 325) or the 40-ampere low cut-in generator (also Option 325) may be used.

Since the real work of steering is done by the power steering mechanism, the overall steering ratio (23.3 to 1) is numerically smaller than that of the regular system. This enables the driver to turn the road wheels with fewer turns of the steering wheel.

Power Cylinder

Pressure Pump

Overall Steering Ratio

CONTROLS

VELVET-PRESSURE
JUMBO-DRUM BRAKES

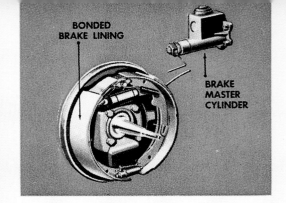

BONDED BRAKE LINING

BRAKE MASTER CYLINDER

Brake Shoes

With hydraulic service brakes, the driver's foot exerts equal pressure at all four wheels causing the brake shoes to contact the brake drums simultaneously. In Chevrolet's design, *all eight* brake shoes (two at each wheel) are self-energized whether the car is going forward or in reverse. This means that little driver effort is required because the turning drums move the brake shoes so that they wedge against the drums. As the shoes move, their linings contact up to 158 sq. in. of the drums' area (total lining area). Because *all four* drums are extra-large (eleven inches inside diameter), Chevrolet brakes are called Jumbo-Drum brakes. The drums are made with steel sides and cast iron braking surfaces that dissipate the heat of braking rapidly. The brake linings, of full-molded asbestos composition for greater heat resistance, are bonded to the brake shoes. With-

Brake Lining Area

Brake Drums

Brake Linings

out rivets, they cannot score the drums and their service life is practically twice as long. Efficient sealing protects them from dirt and splash so all stops are sure.

One of the advantages of Chevrolet's suspended brake pedal is that, with this design, the brake master cylinder is in the engine compartment, high on the dash where it is easily accessible for servicing.

Brake Master Cylinder

PIVOT-PEDAL
POWER BRAKES

Power
Brake
System

Power
Brake
Pedal

Using intake manifold vacuum and atmospheric pressure for its power, the Chevrolet power brake system (Option 412) does up to one-third of the work of stopping. The design is simplicity itself. A vacuum-power cylinder (1) supplies the added power which exerts pressure on (2) the car's hydraulic braking system. A reserve tank (3) assures a vacuum reserve even when the engine is not running. Because this system reduces the distance the brake pedal must travel before the brakes are applied, the pedal is approximately the same height as the accelerator pedal. This enables the driver to shift his toe from one pedal to the other without lifting his heel from the floor. Then, just a gentle toe-tip pressure, and the car stops quietly and smoothly. The brakes work easier, but the driver retains the familiar feel of complete stopping control.

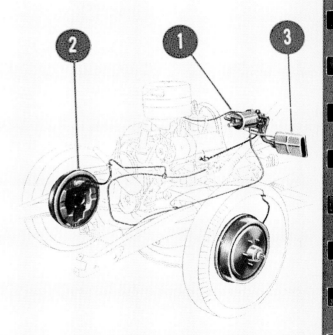

DIRECT-ACTING
PARKING BRAKES

Parking
Brake
System

Because they operate directly on the road wheels and are fully protected from road dirt and splash, the two rear-wheel service brakes are also used as parking brakes. A fully mechanical system, entirely separate from the hydraulic braking system, applies them when the direct-pull T-handle is pulled back. The handle is released by turning it slightly (60° counterclockwise) and pushing it back in. An accessory light, that warns against driving with the brakes on, installs under the instrument panel. It glows red when the ignition is turned on and shines until the brakes are released.

Parking
Brake
Handle

Parking
Brake
Signal

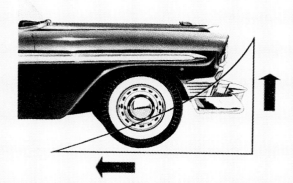

ANTI-DIVE
BRAKING CONTROL

Among the many features pioneered by Chevrolet is controlled braking action by which braking dive is reduced up to 45 percent. This feature is engineered into Chevrolet's spherical-joint front suspension. The scientifically inclined control arms of the suspension produce a lifting effect that counteracts *nosing down* during normal braking to assure *heads up* stops. The result is continued passenger comfort and reduced possibility of locking bumpers in traffic.

Heads Up
Stops

12-VOLT ELECTRICAL SYSTEM

High-Voltage Power Generation
- 25-ampere, 30-ampere** or 40-ampere low cut-in** generators
- 54-plate heavy-duty battery
- Voltage and current regulators

All-Weather Ignition System***
- Solenoid-engaged, high-speed Positive-Shift starter
- Hermetically sealed coil
- High-Tower distributor, with dual automatic spark control
- Sure-firing spark plugs with neoprene caps
- Tightly sealed terminals
- Nonmetallic high-tension cables

Automatic Inside Lights
- Domelight*, courtesy lights*
- Automatic front door* and rear door* inside-light switches
- Automatic glove box light*
- Automatic underhood light**
- Automatic trunk light**

Super-Efficient Driving Lights
- Precision-aimed, sealed-beam headlights, with dual circuit breaker protection
- Extra-large parking lights
- Large taillights; integral stop lights and red reflectors
- Turn-signal lights built into tail and parking lights
- Backup lights in taillights**
- Dual rear license lights
- Built-in or portable spotlights**

Simple Control Switches
- Four-position, key-turn ignition-starter switch
- Master light switch on panel
- Headlight beam foot switch

Electric Driver Aids***
- Two matched vibrator horns
- Powerglide** starter safety switch
- Electric overdrive** engagement
- Electric windshield wipers**
- Red parking brake warning light**

Clear Driving-Control Lights***
- Intensity-controlled white lights for all dials
- Red warning lights for generator charge, oil pressure, and headlight country beams
- Green turn-signal arrows
- Ignition-starter keyhole light
- Heater** or air conditioner** control panel light

Electric Conveniences***
- High-capacity electric blower for heater** or air conditioner**
- Electric power seat adjustment**
- Electric power window controls**
- Hydro-electric convertible top folding mechanism*
- Moisture-sensitive top lift**
- Radio**; instrument panel and auxiliary radio speakers**
- Electric clock*
- Electric cigaret lighter*
- Electric portable shaver**

*See text for models in which feature is furnished.   **Available as optional or accessory equipment.   ***Described in other sections of this book.

12-VOLT POWER . . .
and all the
MODERN ELECTRIC CONVENIENCES!

DOUBLE-PUNCH 12-VOLT ELECTRICAL SYSTEM

The electrical system has gained importance in the past decade, because of the many electrical features that have been added to cars. In addition to starting the engine and keeping it firing, it must perform many services: For safety in modern-day traffic, it must *efficiently power* dual head, tail, stop, parking, turn-signal, backup, and license lights, windshield wipers and horns. For convenience and safety, it must *efficiently power* dome, instrument, control and warning lights. For convenience and comfort, it must *efficiently power* glove, engine, and trunk compartment lights, spotlights, heater or air conditioner blower, seat adjustment, window, and convertible-top controls. And, for convenience and pleasure, it must *efficiently power* a radio, clock, and cigaret lighter.

In 1955, Chevrolet introduced the 12-volt electrical system to the low-price field. With

12 volts, the car's entire electrical system is more efficient than ordinary systems. Not only does it provide superior ignition with quicker starting, more reliable firing, and a hotter spark, but its greater generator efficiency results in less chance of a rundown battery, and extra power to operate all the many electrical features of modern cars.

The efficient, air-cooled generator produces 25 amperes at 12 volts (equal to 50 amperes at six volts) to maintain high battery charge under all driving conditions. For 1956, a larger oil reservoir improves generator lubrication and prolongs the time between refills. A new mounting on V8 engines reduces vibration and lengthens generator life. And new waterproof current and voltage regulators (in a more accessible location on the left fender skirt) assure efficient generator operation at all times. For heavy-duty service, a 30-ampere generator (Option 325) and a 40-ampere low-cut-in generator (also Option 325) are available.

For 1956, Chevrolet's 12-volt system is improved by a new, better, longer lasting battery—warranted by its maker for 36 months, regardless of milage, as compared to the 21-month warranty for the previous battery. Located high under the hood at the right side of the engine for easy servicing, it has 54 plates providing 12 volts (53-ampere-hour rating at 20 hours). Its hard-rubber case is completely resistant to acid absorption, heat, bulging, warping, or other distortion. Even current distribution and a superior resistance to overcharge and corrosion, due to a unique grid design, increase its life nearly 100 percent. Microporous rubber separators—until now found only in the most expensive batteries—not only offer greater resistance to vibration, acid attack, and extremes in temperatures, but also provide improved cranking ability.

Battery

MORE POWERFUL HEADLIGHT LOWER BEAMS

The greater seeing distance down the right side of the road, provided by the lower beams of the new sealed-beam headlights, amounts to as much as 80 feet.

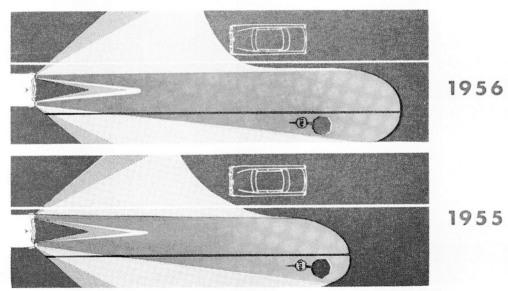

1956

1955

ELECTRICAL

BETTER DRIVING LIGHTS

Headlight Beams

New, improved sealed-beam headlights provide safer driving vision. More powerful upper (*country*) and lower (*city*) beams—50 and 40 watts respectively—provide more light. And the city-beam pattern is designed to give up to 80 feet more seeing distance along the right side of the road where obstacles are most likely to be.

Headlight Reflection Control

For better vision under adverse weather conditions, an improved design of lens and reflector, plus a new opaque city-beam filament shield, bends any stray light downward to minimize reflections from snow, fog, or dust—so they don't reflect back into the driver's eyes. In addition, Chevrolet's distinctive headlight hoods, like canopies above the headlights, shield the lights from snow and drippings that might ice the lenses.

Headlight Aiming

As a field-exclusive feature, three new aiming lugs make it possible for Chevrolet headlights to be aimed with exceptional precision, even when they are unlighted.

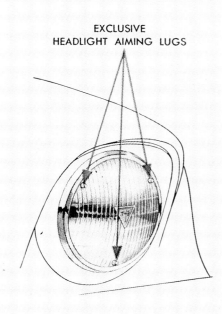

EXCLUSIVE
HEADLIGHT AIMING LUGS

Fast switching from country to city beams, and the reverse, is provided by the convenient foot switch at the left of the toe-panel. An ingenious accessory, *the Autronic Eye*, mounted on top of the instrument panel, does this service automatically. While the country beams are on, the headlight beam indicator in the instrument cluster glows red.

Headlight Beam Switch

Hermetic sealing of the headlights seals out dust, rust, and moisture to assure efficient lighting longer. Moreover, the lights are doubly protected by two circuit breakers that isolate them from shorts in other circuits so they continue to function.

Headlight Protection

For easy, safe guiding of the car at night, both headlights and taillights are mounted high and wide in the fender tops. Not only do they provide nighttime four-fender visibility for easier parking, but they denote the car's exact width to other motorists. When the car lights are off, ruby-red prisms in the taillights glow in the glare of lights of cars approaching from behind.

Head- and Taillight Locations

ELECTRICAL

The taillights are big with prominent conical ruby-red lenses for the taillights and the even brighter stoplights. Not only are they highly visible from the rear but they can be seen by motorists who approach from the sides. Behind white lenses, below the taillight lenses, accessory backup lights

Taillights

light automatically when the car is shifted into reverse. Turn signals, of course, are built into both the parking and taillights. Operated by the lever on the left side of the steering column, the lights on the *turn* side of the car and a corresponding green arrow on the instrument panel flash intermittently. Self-cancellation occurs as turn is completed.

Turn-Signal Lights

The rear license is illuminated by lights neatly built into the bumper guards. An accessory engine compartment light goes on when the hood is raised, as does the accessory trunk light when the trunk lid is lifted.

License Lights, Underhood and Trunk Lights

A powerful accessory sealed-beam spotlight can be aimed in any direction from inside the car. It casts a ray of light up to 1000 feet. A large, optically clear rearview mirror is recessed into the body of the light. The light unit can be installed on either side of the car, or two can be used.

Spotlight

An accessory sealed-beam spotlight, with a 12-foot cord that plugs into the cigaret-lighter socket, also serves as an ideal trouble light that reaches around the car.

Trouble Light

CONVENIENT INSIDE LIGHTS

Dome and Courtesy Lights

In sedans, conventional station wagons, and coupes (except the convertible), there is a central chrome-rimmed domelight. In the Nomad, a similar light is provided above each center pillar. The convertible has two

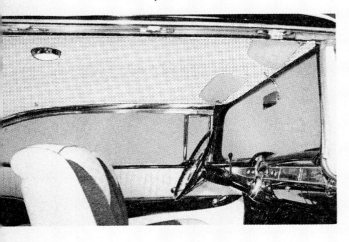

courtesy lights beneath the instrument panel. All these lights have durable plastic lenses.

Nearly all Chevrolets have at least 22 light bulbs—three more than the typical American home. Most of these are manually controlled by the main light switch. It is pulled out to light the driving lights, instrument and radio lights, the keyhole light of the ignition-starter switch, and the control panel light of the accessory de luxe heater or air conditioner. Rotated clockwise, it controls the intensity of the instrument panel lights from a soft white light to complete darkness. Rotated counter-clockwise, it turns on the inside lights. On the Nomad a second switch, at the endgates, also controls the inside lights.

Manual Light Switches

Automatic light switches are provided at all doors of Bel Airs and at the front doors of "Two-Ten" models. When a door is opened, the inside light goes on automatically and stays on until the door is closed. Other automatic light switches include those of the Bel Air and "Two-Ten" glove compartment and accessory underhood and trunk lights.

Automatic Light Switches

ELECTRICAL

ALL THE SUPERIOR VALUES
that contribute to
FULL OWNERSHIP SATISFACTION!

ABBREVIATIONS—av. *average*, cu. ft. *cubic feet*, dia. *diameter*, ft. *feet*, ft-lb *foot-pounds*, gal. *gallons*, hp *horsepower*, lb *pounds*, mm *millimeters*, mph *miles per hour*, opt. *optional*, p or pp *page or pages*, pt. *pints*, qt. *quarts*, rpm *revolutions per minute*, sq. ft. *square feet*, sq. in. *square inches*, std. *standard*, ° *degrees*, " *inches*, % *percent*.

ACCELERATOR—Rubber-padded treadle operates throttle by pushrod through dash panel. Accessory rubber cover with integral heel pad protects floor covering . . . . P 114

ACCESSORIES—Extra-cost equipment installed by dealer on customer's order in addition to or in place of standard equipment. A limited number, installed at factory, are called *factory-installed accessories* . . . . . . Quality P 17, List P 66

AIR CLEANER (Six)—Oil-wetted type, or optional one-pint oil-bath type; each combined with flame arrester and silencer . . . . P 171

AIR CLEANER (V8)—One-pint oil-bath type, with flame arrester and silencer. Special heavy-duty oil-bath type is standard on "Super Turbo-Fire V8" . . . . PP 161, 165

AIR CONDITIONER (V8, except convertible) —Compact, single-unit, all-weather air conditioner by Frigidaire; installs at front of car, leaving trunk space unobstructed . . . . . . P 132

ANTI-DIVE BRAKING—Controlled by front suspension, dive is reduced up to 45% . . . . P 191

APPEARANCE, EXTERIOR . PP 6, 24, 80, 82

APPEARANCE, INTERIOR . . . . P 96

ARMRESTS—Built-in and applied types, with doorpulls when mounted on doors; vinyl cover over foam-rubber pad . . . . P 105

ASHTRAY, INSTRUMENT PANEL—Removable tilting bin with snuffer . . . . P 110

ASHTRAYS, REAR-SEAT—Removable tilting bin with snuffer in front-seat backrest of Bel Air and "Two-Ten" 4-door sedans. Removable bin with snuffer and snap-cover in armrests of Bel Air and "Two-Ten" 2-door sedans, coupes . P 110

ASSIST STRAPS—Two loops aid exit of rear-seat passengers in Bel Air and "Two-Ten" 2-door sedans and "Two-Ten" club coupe . . . . . . P 104

AUTRONIC EYE—Accessory automatic headlight switch (on special order) . . . . P 198

AXLE—Semi-floating type with hypoid drive gears, 2-pinion differential, flanged shafts, and banjo housing with welded-on cover......P 183

AXLE RATIO—3.55 to 1 with automatic transmission, 3.70 to 1 with conventional transmission, 4.11 to 1 with overdrive transmission. Ratios differ to provide rim pull at rear wheels that gives best performance for each power team....P 183

B ◁===▷

BACKUP LIGHTS—Accessory bulbs, behind white lenses in taillights, light automatically when car is shifted into reverse..........P 199

BATTERY—12-volt, 54-plate battery (53 ampere-hour rating at 20 hours); under hood at right side of engine. 36-month warranty...P 195

BATTERY-CHARGE INDICATOR — Red light, at left in instrument cluster, lights when generator is not charging..........PP 109, 194

BEARING AREA—*Circumferential bearing area* is total surface area of bearing, and is same as area of piece of paper wrapped around bearing. *Projected bearing area* is product of bearing's diameter and length. See individual bearings.

BEARINGS, ANTI-FRICTION—Bearings that substitute roll friction for sliding friction: ball bearings, roller bearings, and spherical joints, as in Chevrolet spherical-joint front suspension.

BEARINGS, BABBITT—Babbitt alloy contains high proportions of tin, copper, antimony, and lead which greatly extend its range of service.

BEL AIR MODELS—Basic features .... P 15, List P 26

BELT LINE—Distinctive *dipdown* belt line circumscribes car below windows, as divider between upper body and lower body..............P 92

BODY—Car body is in two sections separated by dash panel. That ahead of dash is *front-end structure;* that behind dash, *body structure.*P 137

BODY BASIC DIFFERENCES............. ....P 11, Chart P 12

BODY BY FISHER QUALITY..........P 11

BODY CONSTRUCTION—Fisher Unisteel (all-steel, all-welded)......P 137, Features list P 134

BODY DRAINAGE HOLES...........P 139

BODY INSULATION—Thorough insulation and sound-deadening of top, floor, dash and cowl, rear-quarter panels, load compartments, wheelhouses, doors, and rear closures..........P 129

BODY MID-BODY FRAME—Comprised of central roof bow, door pillars, and floor cross-beam . . . . P 138

BODY MOUNTING—Many rubber cushions insulate body from chassis. Front-end structure, bolted to body structure, is supported at front on central rubber cushion . . . . P 140

BODY SEALING—Permanent rubber sealing of stationary windows; rubber-backed fabric in window channels; compressed rubber seals around ventipanes, doors, rear closures, front of convertible top. Metal-attached door seals . . . . P 129

BODY SIDES, UNITIZED — Double-walled units, with integral rear fenders . . . . P 139

BODY SILL MOLDINGS—Accessory chrome moldings between wheel openings . . . . P 93

BOLSTERS AND FACINGS, SEAT—All-vinyl. *Bolsters* are those sections of seat upholstery that cover top part of seat backrest and front part of seat cushion. *Facings* cover vertical surfaces at front and sides of cushion and sides of backrest.

BORE AND STROKE—Six 3.56″ x 3.94″, V8 3.75″ x 3.00″. *Bore* of engine cylinder is its inside diameter; *stroke* is distance piston travels up and down in cylinder . . . . Six P 166, V8 P 151

BRAKE DRUMS—11″ dia., cast alloy iron braking surface with cooling ribs; steel web . P 189

BRAKE FEATURES . . . . List P 185

BRAKE LININGS—Full-molded asbestos composition bonded to brake shoes; 158 sq. in. total effective area . . . . P 189

BRAKE MASTER CYLINDER—Mounted on dash panel inside engine compartment . . . . P 189

BRAKE, PARKING—Mechanical actuation of rear-wheel service brakes through steel cables. Direct-pull T-handle control, at left of steering column, is turned 60° counter-clockwise to release brakes . . . . P 191

BRAKE PEDAL — Suspended, rubber-padded pedal . . . . P 114, Power brake pedal P 190

BRAKE SIGNAL, PARKING—Accessory red warning signal, under instrument panel, lights automatically when ignition is turned on and gleams until brakes are released . . . . . PP 109, 191

BRAKES, POWER—Optional low-pedal vacuum-power service-brake control, with pedal on nearly same level of operation as accelerator treadle; vacuum power does up to one-third of work of braking . . . . P 190

BRAKES. SERVICE—4-wheel. Self-energizing brake shoes, actuated by hydraulic pressure equally distributed to four wheel cylinders. P 189

BUMPERS—Chrome, contoured wraparound bumpers with guards. Rear bumper of station wagons is indented at center for mounting license . . . . PP 83, 86, 142

CAMSHAFT (Six)—4-bearing, cast alloy iron shaft driven by gears from crankshaft; 8.14 sq. in. total projected bearing area. High-lift cams for efficient engine *breathing* . . . . P 168

CAMSHAFT (V8)—5-bearing, cast alloy iron shaft driven by chain from crankshaft; 7.3 sq. in. total projected bearing area. High-lift cams for efficient engine *breathing*, with Powerglide and in "Super Turbo-Fire V8" . . . . PP 158, 165

CAMSHAFT BEARINGS—Pressure-lubricated, steel-backed babbitt . . . . Six P 166, V8 P 158

CARBURETOR (Six)—Single-barrel downdraft carburetor with concentric fuel bowl, automatic choke, fast-idle mechanism and warmup de-icing provision . . . . P 171

CARBURETOR, DUAL (V8) — Two-barrel downdraft carburetor with automatic choke, fast-idle mechanism, warmup de-icing provision. P 161

CARBURETOR, FOUR-BARREL ("Super Turbo-Fire V8")—Two dual downdraft carburetors in single unit; two barrels for low and intermediate speeds plus two more for high speeds and acceleration. Automatic choke, fast-idle mechanism, warmup de-icing provision . . . . P 165

CENTER OF GRAVITY—Extra-low. *Center of gravity* is point above road where car weight is concentrated. The lower the center of gravity, the greater the car stability . . . . P 75

CHASSIS—Assembly of frame, springs, power team, wheels, steering system, brakes . . . . . . P 16

CHOKE—Automatic . . . . See Carburetor

CHROME—Chrome-plated or stainless steel appearance parts . . . . Protective features P 95

CIGARET LIGHTER—Electric pop-out type with ash shield on element, in Bel Air and "Two-Ten." Accessory for "One-Fifty" . . . . P 110

CLOCK—Electric, self-starting precision timepiece with sapphire-jeweled movement and illuminated dial; on radio speaker of Bel Air. Accessory for "Two-Ten" and "One-Fifty". P 110

CLUTCH (Six)—Single dry plate type. 9½" dia. facings of molded asbestos composition; 85.2 sq. in. total area. Torsion-dampening coil springs at disk hub. Diaphragm-spring actuation; life-lubricated ball release bearing............P 182

CLUTCH (V8)—Single dry plate type. 10" dia. facings of woven asbestos composition; 100.5 sq. in. total area. Torsion-dampening coil springs at disk hub. Diaphragm-spring actuation for regular V8; actuation by 9 coil springs and 3 pressure levers for "Super Turbo-Fire V8." Life-lubricated ball release bearing......................P 182

CLUTCH, HEAVY-DUTY (Optional for Six and V8)—Single dry plate type. 11" dia. facings of molded asbestos composition; 123.7 sq. in. total area. Torsion-dampening coil springs at disk hub. Diaphragm-spring actuation; life-lubricated ball release bearing............P 182

CLUTCH PEDAL—Suspended; rubber-padded. Not used with automatic transmission ....P 114

COAT HOOKS—Two chrome hooks in rear compartments of Bel Air and "Two-Ten" models, Bel Air convertible and "Two-Ten" Handyman...P 120

COLORS, EXTERIOR—15 colors in choice of 10 solids and 14 two-tones with *speedline* color styling in Bel Air models, or in either conventional or *speedline* color styling in "Two-Ten" and "One-Fifty" models 364 model-color combinations...................Color chart and P 94

COLORS, INTERIOR—Contemporary or Custom-Colored interiors......Color chart and P 99

COMBUSTION CHAMBERS.Six P 167.V8 P 157

COMPACT DESIGN................PP 71, 74

COMPARISON WITH *BIG CAR*........P 79

COMPASS—Accessory lighted compass; mounts in center on top of instrument panel......P 111

COMPRESSION RATIO—8 to 1 (9.25 to 1 for "Super Turbo-Fire V8"). Ratio of volume of gas above piston at bottom of intake stroke to volume of gas above piston at top of compression stroke............Six P 166, V8 PP 157, 165

CONNECTING ROD BEARING AREA (Six) —13.9 sq. in. total projected area.........P 170

CONNECTING ROD BEARING AREA (V8) —13.1 sq. in. total projected area.........P 157

CONNECTING ROD BEARINGS—Pressure-lubricated, precision-replaceable, thin-walled babbitt..........................Six P 170, V8 P 157

CONNECTING RODS—Drop-forged alloy steel of I-section . . . . Six P 170, V8 P 157

CONTROLS, CAR DRIVING . P 113. List P 112

CONVERTIBLE BODY . . . . P 144

COOLING, ENGINE—Cellular radiator, 4-blade fan, ball-bearing water pump, thermostat and by-pass temperature control, water jackets around all cylinders and valve seats. Capacity, 16 qt. (17 with heater) . . . . . Six P 173, V8 P 162

COST PER POUND, RELATIVE . . . . P 76

COURTESY LIGHTS (Convertible) — Two, under instrument panel, light automatically when door is opened. Accessory in other models . . P 200

COWL—Double-walled; reinforced by welded-in dash and instrument panels . . . . P 138

CRANKSHAFT (Six) — 4-bearing, precision-counterbalanced, drop-forged alloy steel shaft; 11.3 sq. in. total projected bearing area . . . . P 168

CRANKSHAFT (V8) — 5-bearing, precision-counterbalanced, drop-forged alloy steel shaft; 9.1 sq. in. total projected bearing area . . . . P 157

CRANKSHAFT BEARINGS — Pressure-lubricated, precision-replaceable, thin-walled, steel-backed babbitt . . . . Six P 168, V8 P 159

CRANKSHAFT VIBRATION DAMPER—Oscillating, rubber-floated type . . Six P 168, V8 P 157

CYLINDER BLOCK (Six)—Cast alloy iron structure containing cylinders in line, cylinder water jackets, upper half of crankcase . . . . . P 166

CYLINDER BLOCK (V8)—Short, rigid, cast alloy iron structure containing two banks of four cylinders, in V arrangement . . . . P 157

CYLINDER HEAD (Six)—Cast alloy iron structure containing integral valve seats and pressed-in steel valve guides. Water passages encircle all seats . . . . P 167

CYLINDER HEADS (V8)—Two, cast alloy iron, containing integral valve seats and guides. Water passages encircle all seats . . . . PP 157, 165

DASH—Wall between engine and passenger compartments (not instrument panel) . . . . P 138

DIFFERENTIAL—2-pinion type. Combination of gears in axle so arranged that turning effort imparted to unit by axle ring gear may be *differentiated*—transmitted at different speeds to each axle shaft so road wheels revolve at different speeds when car is making a turn . . . . P 183

DOORWAY DIMENSIONS—*2-door conventional sedans, club coupe, and conventional station wagons:* 42″ tall x 43.8″ wide below belt and 34″ above belt. *Sport coupe and convertible:* 40″ tall x 43″ wide below belt and 32″ above belt. *Nomad:* 41.5″ tall x 43.8″ below belt and 34″ above belt. *4-door conventional sedans and station wagons:* front door, 42″ tall x 37″ wide below belt, 28″ above belt; rear door, 41″ tall x 27.5″ wide. *4-door sport sedans:* front door 42″ tall x 37″ below belt and 28″ above belt; rear door, 41″ tall x 38″ wide ....Chart P 70

DRIP MOLDINGS—Deep full-length eaves on sides of all models (except convertible) and above rear openings of station wagons ....P 137

ELECTRICAL FEATURES........List P 192
ELECTRICAL SYSTEM—12-volt......P 194
ENGINE (Six)—In-line, valve-in-head design. 140-hp. 8 to 1 compression ratio. 235.5 cu. in. displacement. 3.56″ x 3.94″ bore and stroke . P 166
ENGINE (V8)—90°V, valve-in-head design. 170-hp. with Powerglide; 162-hp. with Synchro-Mesh or Overdrive. 8 to 1 compression ratio. 265 cu. in. displacement. 3.75″ x 3.00″ bore and stroke..................................P 157

ENGINE ("Super Turbo-Fire V8") — 90°V, valve-in-head design. 205-hp. 9.25 to 1 compression ratio. 265 cu. in. displacement. 3.75″ x 3.00″ bore and stroke. 4-barrel carburetor; dual exhausts....................................P 165
ENGINE BALANCING (V8)..........P 163
ENGINE FEATURES, COMPLETE .List P 174
ENGINE FEATURES, NEW........List P 7
ENGINE MOUNTING—Powerplant dynamically balanced on four rubber cushions: two at front and two at rear....................P 173
ENGINE PERFORMANCE...........P 156
ENGINE RPM—Engine speed as measured by the number of crankshaft *revolutions per minute.*
ENGINE WEIGHT—Six, 550 lb. (607 with clutch); V8, 506 lb. (566 with clutch) .....P 77
ENGINEERING, CHEVROLET........P 19
EXHAUST SYSTEM—Single system consisting of exhaust pipe integral with muffler, and full-length tailpipe. On station wagons. tailpipe extends into rear wheel opening behind wheel to prevent fumes entering gateway. Accessory chrome tailpipe extension..........Six P 172, V8 P 162
EXHAUST SYSTEM, DUAL ("Super Turbo-Fire V8").................................P 165

FLOOR SURFACE, STATION WAGON—Durable ribbed linoleum, on load platform, tailgate, and exposed surfaces of folded seat at front of platform . . . . P 119

FLYWHEEL—Cast alloy iron (reinforced pressed steel flywheel in engines used with automatic transmission). Hardened steel ring gear.

FOOT-POUND—Engine torque is measured in pounds of pull at given distance from center of crankshaft, usually one foot; result is *foot-pounds of torque* . . . . See Torque

FOOTRESTS—Solid, comfortably angled front-seat toepan and rear-seat footrest formed in steel floor of body . . . . P 137

FOUR-FENDER VISIBILITY—All four fenders are visible to the seated driver . . . . . . PP 92, 198

FRAME, CHASSIS—Double-drop box-girder frame (with special X-structure of I-beams in convertible) . . . . P 14

FRONT-END STRUCTURE—That portion of body ahead of dash: radiator grille, front fenders, and hood . . . . P 143, Feature list P 135

FUEL GAUGE—Electrically operated dial, in instrument cluster; indirectly lighted . . . . . P 109

FUEL SYSTEM, ENGINE—Pulsator-type fuel pump driven by camshaft, downdraft carburetor, automatic choke, air cleaner, automatic fuel-mixture heat control . . . . . . Six P 171, V8 P 161

FUEL TANK—16-gallon (17, station wagons); large-capacity gasoline filter screen in tank protects fuel system . . . . Six P 171, V8 P 161

FUEL TANK FILLER—Concealed by left taillight, which swings downward. Accessory filler cap with key lock . . . . P 87

GASOLINE—Chevrolet engines operate well on regular grades but, under some conditions, such as high temperature or deposit accumulation, smoother performance may be obtained with premium grades. Compression ratio is high enough to fully utilize higher octane of premium fuel.

GASOLINE, PREMIUM—Gasoline which contains sufficient *ethyl* (tetraethyl lead) to produce an anti-knock or octane rating of 93 or more.

GEAR RATIO—Ratio of number of revolutions one gear requires to turn a larger gear through one complete revolution. Ratio of conventional gears is found by dividing number of teeth in larger gear by number of teeth in smaller gear.

GEAR REDUCTION, TOTAL—Multiplication of transmission gear ratio by axle ratio gives number of revolutions that are made by engine for a single revolution of rear road wheels.

GENERATOR—25-ampere, air-cooled; waterproof current and voltage regulators. Optional 30-ampere. Optional 40-ampere low-cut-in . P 194

GENERATOR used with power steering . . P 188

GLASS—High-quality safety glass . . . . P 129

GLASS, TINTED—Optional green E-Z-Eye safety glass in all windows; shaded band across top of windshield . . . . P 127

GLOVE COMPARTMENT—Fully lined deep compartment with pushbutton key lock, at center of instrument panel . . . . P 110

GLOVE COMPARTMENT LIGHT—Automatic, in Bel Air and "Two-Ten" models; accessory in "One-Fifty" models . . . . P 110

GOVERNOR (Six with 3-speed transmission)—Optional; restricts car speed to 35 miles per hour.

GRAVEL GUARDS—Horizontal splash and gravel guards enclosing spaces between bumpers and body at front and rear of car . . . . P 142

HARMONIC BALANCER—Oscillating, rubber-floated vibration damper mounted on front end of crankshaft . . . . Six P 168, V8 P 157

HATROOM—Interior width at hat level at each seat. Conventional sedans: front 56.0", rear 56.8".

HEADLIGHT BEAM INDICATOR—Red light, in center of speedometer, shines when country beams are on . . . . PP 109, 198

HEADLIGHT FOOT SWITCH—Button at left of toepan is pressed to switch from city beams to country beams and vice versa . . . . P 198

HEADLIGHT HOODS—Hoods, integral with fenders, project beyond lights to shield them from snow and dripping water . . . . PP 83, 197

HEADLIGHTS—Precision-aimed, sealed-beam lights, protected by two circuit breakers; located to denote car width clearly. 50-watt country (upper) beam; 40-watt city (lower) beam. Chrome rims inside headlight hoods . . . . PP 197, 198

HEADLINING—Perforated vinyl in "Two-Ten" club coupe and in Bel Air sport sedan, sport coupe and Nomad; plain vinyl in other station wagons, plain napped cloth in other models.P 101

HEADROOM—Distance from seat cushion to headlining, 5″ ahead of backrest and 8° from vertical. Conventional sedans: front 35.7″, rear 35.4″......Models section and PP 24, 68, 70, 79

HEATER, DE LUXE—Accessory heater and defroster unit controlled from illuminated panel on instrument panel. Heats and circulates inside air or outside air it draws from plenum chamber in double-walled cowl.................P 132

HEATER, RECIRCULATING—Accessory heater and defroster unit, with temperature and defroster controls on instrument panel. Heats and circulates air inside body.............P 132

HEAT GAUGE, ENGINE—Electrically operated dial in instrument cluster.PP 109, 163, 173

HEIGHT, CAR LOADED—*Conventional sedans and club coupe* 60.5″; *sport sedans, sport coupes, and convertible* 59.1″; *Nomad* 59.4″; *other station wagons* 60.8″..Models section and PP 24, 68, 70, 79

HELICAL GEARS—Gears in which teeth are not parallel with gear axis, but set at angle with axis, to provide greater tooth contact surface and quieter gear operation.............P 176

HIPROOM—Width from door to door, measured at cushion level of each seat 5″ ahead of backrest. Conventional sedans: front 62.0″, rear 63.0″......Models section and PP 24, 68, 70, 79

HOOD—Front-opening reinforced one-piece panel with gear-type hinges, double-acting counterbalancing hinge springs, automatic latch with safety catch. Latch, at front slightly to right of center, may be unlatched and hood lifted in one motion....Styling P 85, Construction P 143

HOOD ORNAMENTATION—Colorful plastic emblem in chrome frame, with chrome V on V8 models. Chrome ornament with eagle motif.P 85

HORN CONTROL—Chrome full-circle blowing ring in Bel Air and "Two-Ten"; horn button on steering wheel hub in "One-Fifty".PP 113, 187

HORNS—Two, matched vibrator horns. Accessory trumpet-type vibrator horn with tone blended with those of standard horns.....P 187

HORSEPOWER, MAXIMUM—Six, 140-hp; V8 with Powerglide, 170-hp; V8 with Synchro-Mesh or Overdrive, 162-hp; "Super Turbo-Fire V8," 205-hp. Rate of doing work; measured at rear of crankshaft. One horsepower is developed when work equal to lifting 33,000 lb one foot is done in one minute.............PP 24, 78, 79

HORSEPOWER, POUNDS PER—Car weight divided by max. horsepower . . . PP 24, 68, 78, 79

HOTCHKISS DRIVE—Propeller shaft, with two universal joints, transmits engine turning force from transmission to axle; permits lower body and center of gravity . . . . PP 153, 183

HUB CAPS—Chrome. Chrome full-size wheel disks of Bel Air available as accessories on "Two-Ten" and "One-Fifty" models . . . . P 93

HYDRAULIC POWER—Transference of power, in various forms, through the medium of a fluid.

HYPOID GEARS—Axle drive gear axis is below axis of ring gear permitting ring gear to be made smaller and more durable and drive gear to be made larger and more durable. It also lowers drive train, contributing to lower body and center of gravity and lower car silhouette . . P 183

IGNITION—All-weather type with hermetically sealed coil, high-tower distributor, neoprene spark plug caps. Ignition cable has linen core impregnated with electrical conducting material and insulated with rubber and neoprene jacket . . Six P 172, V8 P 161, Features list P 192

IGNITION-STARTER SWITCH—4-position type (*locked-off, unlocked-off, on,* and *start*) at right of steering column; operated by integral knob or car key. Key-turn starter returns to *on* automatically when released. Keyhole is lighted when car lights are on . . . . P 113

INSIDE ROOMINESS . . . . P 72

INSTRUMENT CLUSTER—High, in front of driver: speedometer, gas gauge, engine-heat indicator, generator-charge, oil-pressure and country-beam warning lights, turn-signal arrows . . . P 109

INSTRUMENT LIGHT—Indirect, soft white light may be dimmed or turned off by turning main light-switch knob. Clock and radio dials have same type of light and same control . P 109

INSTRUMENT PANEL—Welded-in wrap-around panel with central glove compartment, and quadrant-shaped instrument cluster in front of driver, balanced by radio speaker grille of same shape at right . . . . P 107. Feature list P 97

INSTRUMENT PANEL ADDITIONAL EQUIPMENT, BEL AIR—Special chrome insert panel at center, chrome control knobs, automatic glove compartment light, cigaret lighter, and electric clock . . . . P 108

INSTRUMENT PANEL ADDITIONAL EQUIPMENT, "TWO-TEN"—Chrome control knobs, automatic glove compartment light, and cigaret lighter............................P 108

INTAKE MANIFOLD.Six P 172, V8 PP 161, 165

INTERIOR EQUIPMENT COMPARISON, BODY.....................Chart P 120

INTERIOR FABRICS—High-quality pattern cloths and vinyls.........................P 101

INTERIOR FEATURES, NEW.....List P 6

INTERIOR STYLING FEATURES.List P 97

INTERIORS, CONTEMPORARY AND CUSTOM-COLORED....Color chart and P 99

KEY, CAR—Single key, with removable identification-number tab, operates all locks....P 115

LEGROOM—Distance from ball of foot of seated passenger measured on diagonal to edge of seat cushion and horizontally to backrest. Conventional sedans: front 43.1″, rear 40.8″...........
.........Models section and PP 24, 68, 70, 79

LENGTH OVERALL—Sedans and coupes 197.5″, station wagons 200.8″...............
.......Models section and PP 24, 68, 70, 74, 79

LICENSE—*Sedans and coupes,* mounted on trunk lid below handle; *station wagons,* on indentation in center of rear bumper. Lighted by two lights in bumper guards. Accessory chrome frame adjusts to fit all sizes. Special bracket on center of front bumper for front license..........P 86

LIFE EXPECTANCY, CAR............P 23

LIGHTS...Features list P 192, Warning P 109, Driving P 197, Inside P 200

LIGHT SWITCH, MAIN—Knob at left of steering column pulls out to turn on instrument and driving lights; turns clockwise to control instrument light intensity; turns counterclockwise to turn on domelight...............P 200

LIGHT SWITCHES, AUTOMATIC....P 200

LOAD COMPARTMENT FEATURES......
...........................List P 97

LOCKS, KEY—Key locks, with automatic weathershields, for front doors, trunk (or endgates). Key-turn ignition-starter switch. Pushbutton key lock for glove compartment...P 115

LUBRICATION, CHASSIS—Pressure gun . . . .
. . . . P 115

LUBRICATION, ENGINE—Controlled full-
pressure system . . . . Six P 170, V8 P 159

MIRROR, REARVIEW—Universally-adjustable inside type. Accessory mirrors: inside nonglare type, remote-control type (mounts through
left door and is controlled from inside car), universally-adjustable type that can be mounted
outside either door. Another is recessed into
accessory spotlight . . . . P 128

MIRROR, VANITY—Accessory makeup mirror;
clips to back of either sunshade . . . . P 127

MODEL DISTINGUISHING FEATURES . . . .
. . . See individual model pages in Models section

MODEL LIST, COMPLETE . . . . P 26

MODELS ADDED TO LINE . . . . List P 6

MUFFLER, POWER-TONE—30" reverse-flow
muffler with three sound-deadening chambers.
24" muffler in convertible . . . .
. . . . Six P 173, V8 PP 162, 165

NEW CHEVROLET . . . . . Brief Description P 9

OCTANE RATING—Measurement that indi-
cates antiknock properties of gasoline; the higher
the rating, the greater the antiknock properties.

OCTANE SELECTOR—Adjustment at ignition
distributor permits regulation of spark timing to
provide best economy and engine performance
with the grade of gasoline that is used.

OIL CAPACITY—Six—5 qt., V8—4 qt. . . . .
. . . . PP 159, 170

OIL FILLER (Six)—On top of engine at front.
Crankcase breather integral with cap . . . . . P 171

OIL FILLER (V8)—High on left front of engine.
Crankcase breather integral with cap . . . . . P 160

OIL FILTER (Six)—Optional one-quart partial-
flow type oil filter . . . . P 170

OIL FILTER (V8)—Optional one-quart full-
flow type through which *all* oil discharged by
pump must pass before being distributed to
various points of engine . . . . P 160

OIL PAN—Baffle prevents oil-surging on quick stops; reduces oil-foaming...Six P 170, V8 P 160

OIL-PRESSURE LIGHT—In instrument cluster at right; gleams red when pressure is low..P 109

OIL PUMP—High-capacity gear-type oil pump (with cylindrical intake screen) driven by camshaft......................Six P 170, V8 P 160

"ONE-FIFTY" BASIC FEATURES .....P 14

"ONE-FIFTY" MODELS............List P 26

OPTIONAL EQUIPMENT—Extra-cost equipment which is essentially part of the car, installed at factory in addition to or in place of standard equipment.....Quality P 17, List P 66

OVERHANG— Length between bumper and wheel center at each end of car.............P 74

P

PAINT—Polished pyroxylin lacquer.......P 95

PARCEL SHELF—Below window behind rear seat in sedans and coupes except convertible....
......................................P 117

PARKING LIGHTS—Two, in sides of radiator grille below headlights. Chrome rims.......P 83

PASSENGER CAPACITY.....Models section

PERFORMANCE, CAR..................
General descriptions PP 10, 71, 78, 79, 156, 177

PISTON PINS—Chromium-steel pins securely held in connecting rod ends; offset in pistons to insure quiet piston operation..Six P 169, V8 P 157

PISTON RINGS—Two compression rings and one oil control ring.........Six P 169, V8 P 158

PISTONS—Lightweight cast aluminum alloy with integral steel struts to control expansion; surfaces tin-coated to resist wear. Special designs for each engine type.........Six P 169, V8 P 157

PLANETARY GEARS—Gear arrangement in which small gears follow circular path within larger gear and around a center gear......P 179

PLENUM CHAMBER—Air space between inner and outer panels of double-walled cowl....P 131

POWER, INCREASES FOR 1956..Chart P 78

POWER, POSTWAR (1946-1956) PROGRESS IN..................P 23, Chart P 24

POWERPLANT WEIGHT (Six)—611 lb with standard transmission, 639 with overdrive transmission, 708 with automatic transmission...P 77

POWERPLANT WEIGHT (V8)—570 lb with standard transmission, 597 with overdrive transmission, 665 with automatic transmission...P 77

POWER TEAMS—Nine combinations of engines, transmissions, and axles.Chart PP 176-177

PROGRESS, POSTWAR (1946-56) Chevrolet Design....................P 23, Chart P 24

PROPELLER SHAFT—Precision-balanced tubular type; two universal joints...PP 176, 183

QUALITY, CHEVROLET.................P 17

RADIATOR — Ribbed-cellular radiator with pressure cap................Six P 173, V8 P 163

RADIATOR GRILLE—Car-wide chrome lattice-type radiator grille..................P 83

RADIATOR GRILLE GUARD—Accessory chrome grille and front-fender guard; mounts above bumper. Matching guard for rear....P 83

RADIO, MANUAL-TUNING — Accessory 6-tube hand-tuned unit..................P 111

RADIO, PUSHBUTTON — Accessory 7-tube unit operated by five pushbuttons set to predetermined stations..................P 111

RADIO, SIGNAL-SEEKING—Accessory 8-tube unit; automatic tuner bar plus five pushbuttons set to predetermined stations...........P 111

RADIO ANTENNA—Telescoping type, mounted on right front fender; provided with each radio. Accessory adapter for mounting antenna on right rear fender..............P 111

RADIO CONTROLS—Mounted above glove compartment at center of instrument panel.P 111

RADIO SPEAKER GRILLE—Quadrant-shaped; at right side of instrument panel. Decorated with chrome frame, *Bel Air* in gold plate or chrome *Chevrolet*.................PP 107, 109

RADIO SPEAKER, REAR-SEAT—Accessory (6"x9"), mounted flush with parcel shelf...P 111

RAIN DEFLECTORS—Accessory chrome rain-and-sun deflectors installed above side windows of conventional 4-door and 2-door sedans and club coupe.................PP 93, 127

RAMP ANGLES—Angle of approach 25°, angle of departure 15°........PP 24, 68, 74, 79

RECIPROCATING PARTS, ENGINE—Those parts which move up and down within cylinders of engine, namely pistons and connecting rods................Feature List P 174

RIDE, QUADRA-POISE..............P 148

RIM PULL—Turning force at road after engine torque has been transmitted through transmission, axle, wheels, and tires of the car.

ROAD CLEARANCE—8". Height from level road to bottom of axle center with car fully loaded....Models section and PP 24, 68, 75, 79

ROTATING PARTS, ENGINE—Those parts of engine that revolve: crankshaft, crankshaft vibration damper, flywheel, camshaft, and timing gears or chain..............Feature list P 174

RUSTPROOFING—Thorough rustproofing of body and front-end structure before painting. P 95

S ⌁

SASH MOLDINGS—Short chrome moldings on body side rear quarters, extending diagonally down to meet body side moldings..........P 93

SCUFF PADS—Scuff-resistant vinyl panels at bottoms of doors, sidewalls, and front seat; edged with decorative chrome moldings in Bel Air models.

SEAT ADJUSTMENT, FRONT—4.4" total travel, on inclined plane. Chrome pushbutton control at left side of seat riser...........P 106

SEAT ADJUSTMENT, POWER-CONTROLLED FRONT—Optional, automatic electric-power adjustment for Bel Air and "Two-Ten" sedans and coupes................P 106

SEAT BELTS—Accessory on all models..P 105

SEAT CONSTRUCTION—Full-width seats with S-wire springs on all-steel frames, comfortably cushioned, with foam-rubber cushions on front seats of all Bel Air and "Two-Ten" models and on rear seats of all Bel Air sedans, coupes, and Nomad Station Wagon........PP 104, 105

SEAT COVERINGS—Combination of pattern cloth and vinyl, or all-vinyl..............P 101

SEAT COVERS, ACCESSORY—Sets of seat and backrest covers in plastic, nylon or fiber—blue, brown or green—for 4-door and 2-door sedans. Accessory seat cushion covers of transparent nylon-dacron (6 colors) for 4-door and 2-door sedans, sport sedans, sport coupe..P 102

SPARK PLUGS—14-mm; with neoprene caps for protection from moisture. Six P 172, V8 P 161

SPEEDOMETER—High. in front of driver. Adjustable indirect lighting . . . . P 109

SPHERICAL JOINT—Connection in which end of one member is spherical, or partly spherical, and fits in corresponding spherical cavity in another member . . . . PP 151, 186

SPLASH GUARDS—Horizontal metal shields filling spaces between bumpers and body . . P 142

SPORT MODEL BASIC FEATURES . . . P 13

SPORT MODELS AVAILABLE . . . . . List P 27

SPOTLIGHT, PORTABLE—Accessory sealed-beam hand light with 12-foot cord; plugs in cigaret-lighter socket . . . . P 199

SPOTLIGHT, REMOTE-CONTROL—Accessory sealed-beam spotlight with rearview mirror; mounts through body and is controlled from inside car . . . . P 199

STABILITY, CAR . . . . PP 75, 148, 153

STARTER — Solenoid-operated. Positive-Shift starting motor. Key-turn control combined with ignition switch; keyhole lights when car lights are on . . . . P 113, Six P 172, V8 P 161

STATION WAGON BASIC FEATURES . . P 13

STATION WAGON ENDGATE OPENING—
Nomad: 28.4″ tall by 41.8″ wide at belt. *All others:* 28.3″ tall by 43.5″ wide at belt. Height of tailgate from ground (unloaded), approximately 30″ for all models . . . . P 73

STATION WAGON LIFTGATE—High-lifting box-section frame for window; two concealed hinges. Chrome self-latching telescoping supports at sides. Central wedge, engaged by dovetail on tailgate, locks liftgate . . . . P 119

STATION WAGON LOAD SPACE—Flat platform, extended by folding seat, and lowering tailgate. *Nomad:* Capacity 71 cu. ft; length 43″, 74.3″ with seat folded, 97″ with tailgate down; max. width 56.4″. *All others:* Capacity 87 cu. ft; length 47″, 84.4″ with seat folded, 106.1″ with tailgate down; max. width 58.3″ . . . . . PP 73, 119

STATION WAGON TAILGATE—Double-walled steel gate with two hinges. Retractable support cables at sides. Slam latches at sides are operated by central outside chrome handle with key lock. Colorful plastic emblem with chrome frame, plus chrome V on V8s, except on Nomad. Chrome model name and vertical ribs on Nomad, plus chrome Vs on rear fenders of V8s . . . . . P 119

STATION WAGONS AVAILABLE . . List P 27

STEERING COLUMN—Encloses transmission and turn-signal control mechanism. PP 114, 187

STEERING FEATURES . . . . List P 184

STEERING GEAR—Recirculating ball . . P 187

STEERING GEAR RATIO—20 to 1. Ratio of number of steering wheel turns to one turn of pitman arm shaft operating steering linkage P 187

STEERING KNUCKLES—Two self-adjusting spherical joints, with non-metallic liners, at each front wheel . . . . PP 151, 186

STEERING LINKAGE—Relay type. Arrangement of rods, levers, and their articulated joints that connects road wheels to pitman arm . . P 186

STEERING, POWER—Optional hydraulic-power steering control. Assistance starts at 3 pounds steering wheel rim pull; reaches 80% at 8 pounds . . . . P 187

STEERING RATIO, OVERALL—25.7 to 1 (23.3 to 1, power steering). Ratio of number of turns of steering wheel to angular turn of front road wheels . . . . Standard P 186, Power P 188

STEERING WHEEL—18" dia., steel-reinforced hard rubber wheel (3-spoke in Bel Air, 2-spoke in "Two-Ten" and "One-Fifty") . . . PP 113, 187

STYLING . . . . Front P 83, Side P 90, Rear P 86

SUNSHADES—Universally-adjustable. Two in Bel Air and "Two-Ten" models; one in "One-Fifty" models with second as accessory . . . . Coverings P 101, Operation P 125

SUN VISOR, OUTSIDE—Accessory metal visor painted to match car and edged with chrome molding; for all models except convertible. P 127

SUSPENSION FEATURES . Lists PP 146, 147

SUSPENSION, FRONT—Independent wheel suspension with coil springs of chrome alloy steel; shock absorbers inside springs. Self-adjusting spherical joints with non-metallic liners at wheels. Four lubrication fittings . . . . P 150

SUSPENSION, REAR—Longitudinal, chrome alloy steel, semi-elliptic leaf springs, 58" long by 2" wide, 46" spring centers. Number of leaves varies for different models. Optional springs for heavy-duty service. Lubrication-eliminating leaf-end inserts. Outrigger mounting with compression shackles. Diagonal shock absorbers . . . P 153

TAILLIGHTS—Ruby-red lens for tail, stop, and turn-signal lights; white lens for accessory backup lights; red reflex buttons. Chrome frames. Broad spacing of lights in top of rear fenders denotes car width in dark...... PP 87, 198, 199

THERMOSTAT, COOLING SYSTEM—Bellows type, in cylinder head water outlet.

TIMING CHAIN (V8)—Silent chain and sprocket drive...................... P 158

TIMING GEARS (Six)—Helical gears: fabric composition drive gear, steel driven gear .. P 168

TIRES—Extra-low-pressure tubeless tires: 6.70-15, 4-ply rating (6-ply rating on 9-passenger station wagons). Optional 6.70-15, 6-ply rating and 7.10-15, 4-ply rating tires. 24-pound inflation pressure for 4-ply (cold); 30-pound pressure for 6-ply (cold). All sizes available with optional white sidewalls...................... P 149

TIRE STOWAGE—*Sedans and coupes:* Inclined in well in right side of trunk; accessory Continental outside carrier. *Station wagons:* In well below load platform; section of platform lifts out for access to spare wheel...... PP 116, 117, 119

TIRE TOOLS—Bumper-jack; 1200-lb capacity. Jack handle combined with wheel wrench. Rattle-free stowage with spare tire. Accessory tool kit with bag.................. P 149

TISSUE DISPENSER—Accessory pivoting box, with chrome front; mounts below instrument panel; holds standard size box of tissues... P 111

TOP, CONVERTIBLE—Folding top of vinyl-coated chevrolon (special weatherproof fabric) in blue, ivory, tan, or black with zippered-in vinyl-plastic rear window; tailored to all-steel articulating framework. Folds completely into well behind rear seat and is covered by snapped-on vinyl boot that matches seat upholstery. Has automatic hydraulically operated folding mechanism controlled from instrument panel....
.... P 144

TOP LIFT, CONVERTIBLE — Accessory moisture-sensitive raiser lifts and unfolds top automatically when rain starts............ P 144

TOP, TURRET—One-piece all-steel top reinforced by central roof bow (two in conventional station wagons) and box-section siderails; integral drip moldings at sides of all models (except convertible) and above rear gateway of station wagons...... Styling P 91, Construction P 137

TORQUE—Engine torque (power to turn) is product of engine force multiplied by distance in feet at which it is exerted from center of crankshaft.................See Foot-pound

TRAFFIC LIGHT VIEWER—Accessory prism unit; mounts on top of instrument panel; shows traffic light in true colors when direct view of light through windshield is blocked......P 127

TRANSMISSION, AUTOMATIC (POWER-GLIDE)—Optional 3-element hydraulic torque converter, with planetary gears for reverse and low. Selector lever on steering column. Lighted selector indicator (with P-N-D-L-R sequence) in instrument cluster. Safety switch in starter circuit. Oil cooler integrated with engine cooling system. Ratios: Maximum torque-converter ratio 2.10 to 1, planetary-gear ratio 1.82 to 1, maximum overall ratio 3.82 to 1.................P 179

TRANSMISSION, CONVENTIONAL—Heavy-duty 3-speed Synchro-Mesh transmission with gearshift lever on steering column. Gear ratios: first 2.94 to 1, second 1.68 to 1, third 1.00 to 1, reverse 2.94 to 1. In synchro-mesh transmission, teeth of high and second-speed gears are constantly meshed and sliding clutches are used to activate gears.................P 181

TRANSMISSION, OVERDRIVE—Optional 3-pinion planetary-gear overdrive, combined with Synchro-Mesh transmission, provides additional forward gear in which engine speed is reduced more than 22% for same road speed as with conventional transmission. Gear ratio .70 to 1. Accelerator control: electric cut-in by releasing treadle at approximately 30 mph; downshift to direct drive by pressing treadle to floor. Handle, at right of steering column, is pulled out to disengage overdrive.................P 180

TREADS, WHEEL—Front 58.0″, rear 58.8″. Tread is width across car at road level between tire centers.................PP 24, 68, 75, 79

TRUNK (Sedans and coupes)—20 cu. ft. capacity (17 convertible). Extra-low sill. Black rubber floor mat.................
.........P 116, Dimensions P 72, Styling P 88

TRUNK LID—Double-walled lid with concealed, full-travel, torque-rod type counter-balancing hinges that cannot interfere with or damage luggage. Stationary chrome handle combined with plastic emblem (plus chrome V on V8s; key lock below handle. Lid locks, without use of key, when shut.................P 116

VALVE TRAIN (Six)—Silichrome steel intake valves, aluminum-dipped extra-alloy steel exhaust valves. Close-grained cast iron valve guides pressed in cylinder head. Valve seats integral with head. Variable-pitch valve springs. Armasteel rocker arms operating on common shaft. Solid upset-ended pushrods. Hydraulic valve lifters . . . . P 169

VALVE TRAIN (V8)—Silichrome steel intake valves, aluminum-dipped extra-alloy steel exhaust valves. Valve guides and seats integral with cylinder heads. Variable-pitch valve springs. Independent pressed steel rocker arms. Hollow pushrods carrying oil to rocker arms. Hydraulic valve lifters . . . . PP 158, 159

VENTILATION, ENGINE—Road draft at end of ventilator tube sucks fumes from engine; exhausts them below car . . . . Six P 171, V8 P 160

VENTILATION, HIGH-LEVEL—Air intake through five banks of louvers in top of cowl. Shroud-length plenum chamber in double-walled cowl, with water drainage to ground. Large outlet louvers in cowl sides direct air toward body level and toward floor. Pull-out knobs on instrument panel ends control outlets . . . . P 130

VENTILATION, NO-DRAFT—Crank-operated, pivoting, chrome-framed ventipanes (with sliding bolt locks) in front doors . . . . PP 130, 131

VENTILATION-HEATING FEATURES . . . . P 122

VIBRATION ELIMINATION—Isolation of all driving controls from engine and road sensations . . . . P 148

VINYL—Vinyl plastic on cloth backing; provides durable and washable, colorful material of pleasing design . . . . P 101

VISION AREA—Conventional sedans 24.4 sq ft . . . . Models section and PP 24, 70, 72

VISION, DRIVING . . . . P 125

VISION FEATURES . . . . List P 122

VOLTAGE AND CURRENT REGULATORS—Waterproof; on left fender skirt in engine compartment . . . . P 194

WATER JACKETS, CYLINDER—Full-length jacket around each cylinder . Six P 166, V8 P 163

WATER PASSAGES, VALVE—Seats are encircled with water, eliminating any need for special inserts . . . . Six P 173, V8 P 163